To Our Readers

Changes: Readers of this publication are encouraged to submit suggestions and changes that will improve it. Recommendations may be sent directly to Commanding General, Doctrine Division (C 42), Marine Corps Combat Development Command, 3300 Russell Road, Suite 318A, Quantico, VA 22134-5021 or by fax to 703-784-2917 (DSN 278-2917) or by E-mail to **smb@doctrine div@mccdc**. Recommendations should include the following information:

- Location of change
    Publication number and title
    Current page number
    Paragraph number (if applicable)
    Line number
    Figure or table number (if applicable)
- Nature of change
    Add, delete
    Proposed new text, preferably double-spaced and typewritten
- Justification and/or source of change

Additional copies: A printed copy of this publication may be obtained from Marine Corps Logistics Base, Albany, GA 31704-5001, by following the instructions in MCBul 5600, *Marine Corps Doctrinal Publications Status.* An electronic copy may be obtained from the Doctrine Division, MCCDC, world wide web home page which is found at the following universal reference locator: **http://ismo-www1.quantico.usmc.mil/docdiv**.

**Unless otherwise stated, whenever the masculine or feminine
gender is used, both men and women are included.**

DEPARTMENT OF THE NAVY
Headquarters United States Marine Corps
Washington, DC 20380-1775

3 October 1997

FOREWORD

Marine Corps Reference Publication (MCRP) 3-17B, *Engineer Forms and Reports,*
provides Marine air-ground task force (MAGTF) engineers with authoritative formats
of engineer-related reports, annexes, appendices, tabs, and enclosures normally
required in operation plans and orders. This publication complements Fleet Marine
Force Manual (FMFM) 13, *MAGTF Engineer Operations*, and provides a complete
foundation for the execution of engineer operations. The primary target audience is all
engineers responsible for executing and reporting engineer support to the MAGTF.

Reviewed and approved this date.

BY DIRECTION OF THE COMMANDANT OF THE MARINE CORPS

J. E. RHODES
Lieutenant General, U.S. Marine Corps
Commanding General
Marine Corps Combat Development Command

DISTRIBUTION: 144 000032 00

TABLE OF CONTENTS

SECTION 1

GENERAL

Forms and Reports   Page

Daily Engineer Situation Report

Copy no.____of copies____
Issuing headquarters
PLACE OF ISSUE
Date/time of issue

Engineer Situation Report No.____ for period_____to_____ 19_____

Ref: (a) Map: Sheet, Series, Scale
    (b)
    (c)

1. ENEMY INFORMATION

Report enemy information which is relevant to engineer operations. Information in this paragraph may be of intelligence or historical value.

2. ENGINEER PERSONNEL

Report attachments and detachments affected during the reporting periods; as well as casualties, noneffectives, and other personnel matters of importance. The term engineer personnel refers to personnel organic to the unit, without regard to MOS.

3. ENGINEER DIFFICULTIES

Report all difficulties that have a bearing on engineer operations.

4. WEATHER

A general statement of weather conditions during this reporting period.

5. OPERATIONS

Verbal highlights.

a. Project Number. Projects assigned by the battalion will be designated by a number such as Abatis-F:1/3:1A/1CEB:U:002. This number indicates a friendly abatis in 1/3's zone emplaced by 1st Plt, A Co., 1stCEB, under construction, and is the second abatis being constructed by 1st Platoon.

b. Description. A short description of the project, such as bridge construction, minefield clearance, road construction, etc.

c. Location. Use map coordinates or other common reference.

d. Starting Time/Date. Enter the time and date that each project was initiated.

e. Percent Completed. Enter an estimate of the percentage of the overall project completed.

(Page number)

Daily Engineer Situation Report—Continued

CLASSIFICATION

f. Estimated Time/Date of Completion. Include the estimated time and date of completion of each project on each report. This entry should be reevaluated for each reporting period to provide the best possible estimate.

g. Continuation Sheet. When the operations block does not provide sufficient space, attach continuation sheets 1-A, 1-B, etc.

Example of table structure:

Project Number	Description	Location	Starting Time/Date	Percent Completed	Estimated Time/Date Completion

6. EQUIPMENT STATUS

Include the following information:

a. Identify equipment deadlined and reason.

b. Equipment attached and detached since last report.

c. POL status.

7. CONSTRUCTION MATERIAL

List the status of critical construction materials by project number. The following may be used as a guide.

Project Number	Item & Qty on Hand	Qty Required Next 24 Hrs	Required for Completion By

8. ENGINEER INTELLIGENCE INFORMATION

List all items of engineer intelligence collected during the period.

9. GENERAL ENGINEER COMMENTS

Report any items deemed appropriate, but not included in other paragraphs.

10. COMMAND POST LOCATION IF CHANGED FROM LAST REPORT

Report only location changes since last report.

Signature
Grade   Service

(Page number)

CLASSIFICATION

Fragmentary Engineer Situation Report and Engineer Equipment Report

FRAGMENTARY ENGINEER SITUATION REPORT

ALPHA	Subject of the Frag Sit Rep, such as enemy minefield.
BRAVO	Location of the subject.
CHARLIE	Time germane to the subject, not the time message is sent.
DELTA	Action desired or support requested.
ECHO	Action taken by the reporting unit.
FOXTROT	Any other additional pertinent information.

ENGINEER EQUIPMENT REPORT
(To cover static and mobile mechanical equipment.)

ALPHA	Map sheet(s).
BRAVO	Data and time of collection of information.
CHARLIE	Location (grid reference or trace).
DELTA	Type of equipment.
ECHO	Number on hand.
FOXTROT	Condition of equipment.
GOLF	Any other information which could be given.

Engineer Reconnaissance Instructions

ENGINEER RECONNAISSANCE INSTRUCTIONS

NO.____

From: _____
(Organization)

To:_____ Effective: ____,_____ (Date-time group)

Maps: _____

Completed report to_____at___._____
(Organization)   (Place, Time, and Date)

Reconnoiter and report information as indicated by items checked below. Also report any other information of technical importance discovered.

DETAILED INSTRUCTIONS: Areas, special features of structures encountered. Estimates of work are required.

---

1. **ROADS:** classify using symbols.

2. **BRIDGES, FORDS AND FERRIES**: classify using symbols. Possible bypass for existing crossings.

3. **OBSTACLES TO OUR MOVEMENT:** natural and artificial including demolitions, mines, boobytraps.

4. **TERRAIN:** general nature, ridge system, drainage system including fordability, forests, swamps, areas suitable for mechanized operations.

5. **ENGR MATERIALS:** particularly road material, bridge timbers, lumber, steel, explosives.

Engineer Reconnaissance Instructions—Continued

ENGINEER RECONNAISSANCE INSTRUCTIONS

6. **ENGR EQUIPMENT:** rock crushers, sawmills, garages, machine shops, blacksmith shops, etc.

7. **ERRORS AND OMISSIONS ON MAPS USED.**

8. **BARRIERS TO ENEMY MOVEMENT:** natural, artificial and sites for construction of improvement (work estimates).

9. **WATER POINTS:** recommended locations.

10. **STREAMS:** general description, width, depth, banks, approaches, character of bottom, means to be used at possible crossing sites, navigability.

11. **DEFENSIVE POSITIONS.**

12. **BIVOUAC AREAS:** entrances, soil, drainage, sanitation, concealment.

13. **PETROLEUM STORAGE AND EQUIPMENT.**

14. **UTILITIES:** water, sewage, electricity, gas.

15. **PORTS:** wharves, sunken obstacles, cargo handling facilities, storage facilities, transportation routes.

16. **CONSTRUCTION SITES:** drainage, water supply, power sources, earthwork, access, acreage, soil.

17. **OTHER:**

Engineer Reconnaissance Report, DA Form 1711-R

ENGINEER RECONNAISSANCE REPORT For use of this form, see FM 5-36; the proponent is TRADOC	PAGE ____ OF ____ PAGES	

TO	FROM

FILE NO	PARTY LEADER (Name, Grade, Unit)	PLACE-HOUR-DATE
REPORT NO		

MAPS	SCALE

DELIVER TO (Organization, Place, Hour and Date)

KEY	OBJECT	TIME OBSERVED	WORK ESTIMATE	ADDITIONAL REMARKS AND SKETCH

Engineer Work Estimate On The Other Side

TYPED NAME, GRADE, ORGANIZATION	SIGNATURE

DA Form 1711-R, May 85   Edition of 1 Jun 61 is obsolete

Engineer Reconnaissance Report, DA Form 1711-R—Continued

ENGINEER WORK ESTIMATE									
LOCATION KEY	DESCRIPTION OF WORK	UNIT RE-QUIRED	NO HOURS	EQUIPMENT			MATERIALS		
				TYPE	NO	HOURS	TYPE	UNIT	QUANTITY

Page 2, DA Form 1711-R, May 85

Reconnaissance Report on Other Side

Enemy Stores and Equipment Report, Installation Report, and Local Resources Report

ENEMY STORES AND EQUIPMENT REPORT

ALPHA	Map sheet(s).
BRAVO	Date and time information was collected.
CHARLIE	Location (grid coordinates).
DELTA	Type (ammunition, vehicle).
ECHO	Quantity.
FOXTROT	Condition.
GOLF	Additional information.

INSTALLATION REPORT

ALPHA	Map sheet(s).
BRAVO	Date and time information was collected.
CHARLIE	Location (grid coordinates).
DELTA	Type of installation.
ECHO	Capacity, including shelter or storage.
FOXTROT	Condition.
GOLF	Additional information.

LOCAL RESOURCES REPORT

ALPHA	Map sheet(s).
BRAVO	Date and time information was collected.
CHARLIE	Location (grid coordinates).
DELTA	Type.
ECHO	Quantity of stock.
FOXTROT	Capacity and/or output per day.
GOLF	Additional information.

Terrain Report and Water Point Report

TERRAIN REPORT

ALPHA	Map sheet and grid references (four grid coordinates to outline area reconnoitered).
BRAVO	Shape of the ground, for example, flat, rolling, hilly, swampland, or mountainous.
CHARLIE	Cross-country movement (GO, SLOW-GO, or NO GO).
DELTA	Vegetation (type and restrictions, if any).
ECHO	Concealment available.
FOXTROT	Land use (rice paddies, plowed but unplanted, wheat fields, and so forth).
GOLF	Suitability of soil for digging, for example, good (no rocks), poor (rocky, clay), and difficult—depending on existing weather conditions.
HOTEL	Weather at time of report (dry, wet, frozen, etc.).

WATER POINT REPORT

ALPHA	Map sheet(s).
BRAVO	Date and time information was collected.
CHARLIE	Location (grid coordinates).
DELTA	Type (well, spring, watercourse, lake, pond).
ECHO	Rate of delivery of water.
FOXTROT	Total quantity of water available and description of water source (salty, clear, muddy, polluted, etc.).
GOLF	Existing pumping and storage facilities.
HOTEL	Accessibility.
INDIA	Additional information.

SECTION 2

MOBILITY

Airfield Report and Air Landing Area Report

AIRFIELD REPORT

ALPHA	Map sheet(s).
BRAVO	Date and time information was collected.
CHARLIE	Location (grid coordinates).
DELTA	Number of runway(s) (length and width).
ECHO	Orientation of runway(s).
FOXTROT	Type and surface of runway(s).
GOLF	Condition of runway(s).
HOTEL	Hangars and bulk fuel storage facilities, including condition.
INDIA	Aircraft parking areas.
JULIETT	Maintenance facilities.
KILO	Road access(es).
LIMA	Any other information.

AIR LANDING AREA REPORT

ALPHA	Map sheet(s).
BRAVO	Date and time information was collected.
CHARLIE	Location (grid coordinates).
DELTA	Runway(s), (1) Bearing, (2) Length and width, (3) Gradients exceeding standards, (4) Rough estimate of earthwork required, (5) Feasibility of runway extension.
ECHO	Drainage.
FOXTROT	Major obstacles to flying, (1) Within approach zone, (2) Outside approach zone, but within 5 miles.
GOLF	Type of soil.
HOTEL	Availability of areas suitable for dispersal.
INDIA	Local resources.
JULIETT	Approach roads.

Airstrip Report and Amphibious Crossing Site Report

AIRSTRIP REPORT

ALPHA	Map sheet(s).
BRAVO	Date and time information was collected.
CHARLIE	Location (grid reference).
DELTA	Dimensions.
ECHO	Type and condition of the facility. Also type and condition of possible helicopter landing zones and LAPES sites.
FOXTROT	Access by road.
GOLF	Feasibility of expansion (or airstrip extension).
HOTEL	Any other information that could be provided such as work required to make the facility serviceable for sustained limited operations.

AMPHIBIOUS CROSSING SITE REPORT

ALPHA	Map sheet(s).
BRAVO	Date and time information was collected.
CHARLIE	Location (grid coordinates).
DELTA	Types of amphibious vehicles considered (AAV, LAV, etc.).
ECHO	Classification and frontage, in meters, of complete site; for example, WHITE-400 meters. _ White. A site where vehicles can be expected to make a passage with such ease that few, if any, will require assistance. _ Gray. A site where the majority of vehicles will require assistance to make a passage. _ Black. An impractical site owing to the excessive amount of assistance required.
FOXTROT	General information of other limitations, such as, mines, debris, ice flows, ice thickness, enemy observation, enemy fire, and explanation of restrictive factors.

Classification Bridge Assessment Summary Form

CLASSIFICATION BRIDGE ASSESSMENT

START PT:
END PT: _____ OF _____

BRIDGE # BYPASS	LOCATION MIL GRID	MLC EXST/IMP	LGTH (M)/ SPANS ()	BATTLE DAMAGE	SOLUTION	TIME REQUIRED
EXAMPLE:						
1 IMPOSS	AB 123456	50/70	45M/3	1 SPAN	MGB	1.5 HOURS

Classification Bridge Assessment Summary Form

Breach Comparison

BREACH COMPARISON

	In Stride	Deliberate	Assault	Covert
Enemy Situation	Unclear or obstacle lightly defended	Situation clear and/or obstacle heavily defended or complex	Enemy has protective obstacles; primary threat is small arms	Situation clear; tactical obstacles bypassable; surprise critical to success
Recon	Quick; may be done during the attack	Extensive recon; detailed obstacle intel; verify enemy positions and obstacles	Recon of protective obstacles may be limited to verifying presence only	Extensive recon; detailed obstacle intel; obstacle composition critical
Planning	Focus on allocating resources to subordinates	Mass drives task org and synchronization drives planning	Task org focuses on assaulting platoons	Mass drives task org; synch critical; plan must achieve surprise
Synchronization	SOSR synchronized at the sub unit level	SOSR synchronized by the commander	SOSR at two levels: Platoon: Point of penetration TF: Isolate the objective area	SOSR synchronized by the commander; obscure thru stealth secure and reduce/suppress only during assault
Reserve Plans	Maintain mobility reserve; plan for transition to deliberate breach	Small engineer reserve; be prepared to commit to breach or improve lanes	No immediate reserve at assaulting platoon level	Be prepared to deliberate breach if detected; support force fires, engineers resort to explosive reduction
Engineer Task Organization	Decentralized; redundant/diverse assets forward; mobility reserve	Centralized; redundant/diverse assets massed in breach force echelon	Very decentralized; assets task organized down to maneuver platoons/squads	Centralized; assets massed in breach/security force
Rehearsals	Focus on sub unit; emphasize cross training	Multi-echelon; train specific tasks and synchronization	Focus on platoon, squad, and fire team	Same as deliberate; must replicate limited visibility

Bridge Reconnaissance Report, DA Form 1249

BRIDGE RECONNAISSANCE REPORT For use of this form, see FM 5-36; the proponent agency is USCONARC.			DATE	SIGNATURE	
TO: *(Headquarters ordering reconnaissance)*			FROM: *(Name, grade, and unit of officer or NCO making reconnaissance)*		
MAPS *(Country, scale, and sheet number or name)*			DATE/TIME GROUP *(Of signature)*		

ESSENTIAL BRIDGE INFORMATION								ADDITIONAL BRIDGE INFORMATION
		CLEARANCE		SPANS				*(Add columns as needed)* *(Military load class, overall length, roadway width, vertical clearance, bridge by-pass)*
	LOCATION						LENGTH AND CONDITION	
1	2	3	4	5	6	7	8	

DA FORM **1249**   PREVIOUS EDITION OF THIS FORM IS OBSOLETE.
1 JUL 60

Bridge Reconnaissance Report, DA Form 1249—Continued

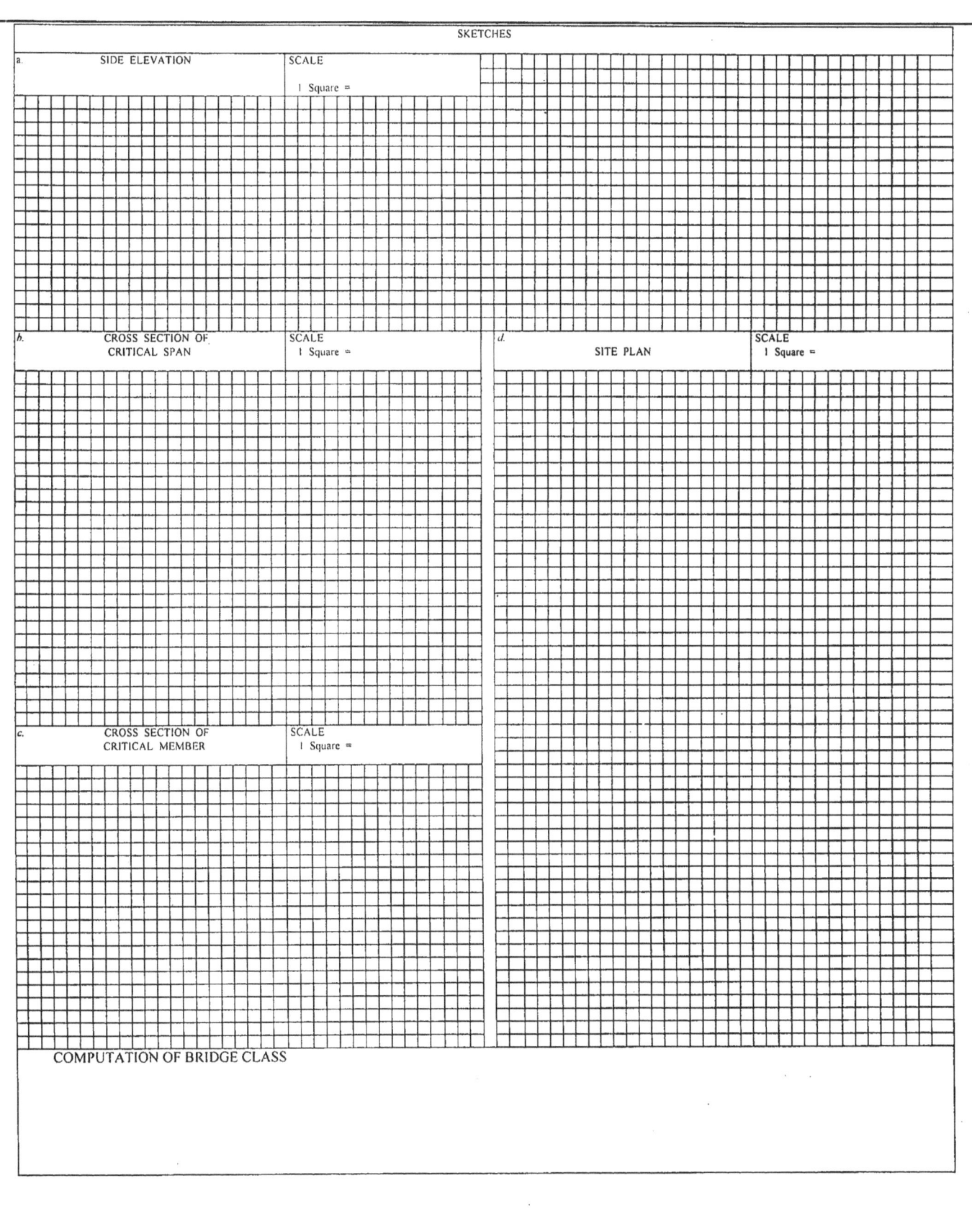

Bridge Report and Bridge Site Report

BRIDGE REPORT

ALPHA	Map sheet(s).
BRAVO	Date and time information was collected.
CHARLIE	Location (grid reference).
DELTA	Type of bridge (number of spans, length, and type of material).
ECHO	Military load classification (one-way traffic). (if known)
FOXTROT	Military load classification (two-way traffic). (if known)
GOLF	Condition of bridge.
HOTEL	Clearance width for vehicle passage.
INDIA	Clearance height for vehicle passage.
JULIETT	Possible bypass route(s) and condition of bypass (difficult or easy).
KILO	Any other information which could impact on trafficability, for example, bridge is prepared for demolition, type and condition of abutments.

BRIDGE SITE REPORT

ALPHA	Map sheet(s).
BRAVO	Date and time information was collected.
CHARLIE	Location (grid reference or overlay).
DELTA	Width of gap between near and far bank edge of gap.
ECHO	Width at water level.
FOXTROT	Width at bottom of gap.
GOLF	Rise and fall of water level and change in wet gap width.
HOTEL	Velocity of current.
INDIA	Nature of bottom.
JULIETT	Height of near bank above water level.
KILO	Height of far bank above water level.
LIMA	Safe bearing pressure of soil.
MIKE	Description of work required on approaches, both near and far banks.
NOVEMBER	Possible local areas for concealing bridging equipment.
OSCAR	Potential staging areas.
PAPA	Turnouts for oversize, overweight, or disabled vehicles.
QUEBEC	Trafficability.
ROMEO	Road nets.
SIERRA	Assembly areas.
TANGO	Engineer release point.

Combat Route Site Report and Dam and Sluice Report

COMBAT ROUTE SITE REPORT

ALPHA	Map sheet.
BRAVO	Date-time group of reconnaissance.
CHARLIE	Location (grid coordinates, or show on overlay).
DELTA	Type of combat route required (TRAIL or ROAD).
ECHO	Type of vehicles considered (wheeled or tracked) and anticipated traffic (light, moderate, heavy); for example, WHEELED-MODERATE.
FOXTROT	Classification and length (in meters) of complete site; for example, GRAY-200 meters. _ White. A site where a minimum of engineer effort is required due to suitable soils, existing grades, and sparse vegetation clearing requirements. _ Gray. A site where a concentrated engineer construction effort is required to produce the required trafficway. Heavy clearing, soil stabilization, and the provision of drainage structures are examples of work required. Vehicles may still require assistance to negotiate steep grades. _ Black. An impractical combat route site owing to the excessive amount of assistance required.
GOLF	General information to include other limitations; for example, mines, enemy observation, enemy fire, existing or reinforcing nonmine obstacles.

DAM AND SLUICE REPORT

ALPHA	Map sheet(s).
BRAVO	Date and time information was collected.
CHARLIE	Location (grid coordinates).
DELTA	Types (concrete, earthen, etc.).
ECHO	Dimensions (length, height, thickness at top and bottom).
FOXTROT	Condition.
GOLF	Additional information.

Demolition Reconnaissance Record, DA Form 2203-R

DEMOLITION RECONNAISSANCE RECORD
For use of this form see FM 5-250; the proponent agency is TRADOC.

SECTION I - GENERAL

			NAME AND RANK	ORGANIZATION
1. FILE NO.				
2. DEMOLITION RECON REPORT NO.	5	RECON ORDERED BY		
3. DATE	4. TIME	6	PARTY LEADER	

7. MAP INFORMATION

Name

Scale

Sheet No.

Series No.

11. GENERAL DESCRIPTION: (Attach sketches)

Type Construction
☐ Earth
☐ Timber
☐ Concrete
☐ Steel

Other Data
☐ Roadway width _____
☐ Number bridge spans _____
☐ Number of lanes _____
☐ Bridge Class: W- _____ T- _____

Condition
_____
_____
_____
_____

8. TARGET AND LOCATION

12. NATURE OF PROPOSED DEMOLITION (Attach sketches.)

9. TIME OBSERVED

10. COORDINATES

13. UNUSUAL FEATURES OF SITE:
☐ High Tension ☐ _____
☐ Radar Installation ☐ _____
☐ Underwater Blasting ☐ _____

SECTION II - ESTIMATES

Determine availability of Items 14, 15, and 16 before conducting reconnaissance.

14. MATERIAL REQUIRED	UNIT OF ISSUE	TYPE MISSION		
		CRATERING	CUTTING	OTHER/SPEC PURPOSE
Electric caps	EA			
Nonelectric caps	EA			
Detonating cord	FT			
Time Fuse	FT			
Fuse Lighters	EA			
Firing Wire	FT			
Firing Device (Specify type.)	EA			
Explosive:				
TNT, 1/4 - LB	EA			
TNT, 1/2 - LB	EA			
TNT, 1 - LB	EA			
TNT, 2 1/4 - LB	EA			
(Other)				
(Other)				
Cratering:				
Cratering Charge, 40 - LB	EA			
Shape Charge, 15 - LB	EA			
Shape Charge, 40 - LB	EA			
M180	EA			
Other Demolitions				

15. EQUIPMENT AND TRANSPORT REQUIRED (*Examples: trucks, ram sets and cartridges, demolition sets, post-hole diggers, nails, adhesives, tape, sandbags, and lumber.*)
NOTE: Troops may not ride in vehicles transporting explosives.

16. PERSONNEL AND TIME REQUIRED FOR:	NCOs	ENL	Time
a. Preparing and placing charges			
b. Arming and firing demolition			

17. TIME, LABOR, AND EQUIPMENT REQUIRED FOR BYPASS (*Specify location and method. Specify equipment to clear the site after demolition and the available bypasses that allow units to bypass the site.*)

18. REMARKS

DA Form 2203-R, MAY 92   Edition of Aug 70 is obsolete.

Demolition Reconnaissance Record, DA Form 2203-R—Continued

DEMOLITION RECONNAISSANCE RECORD
Place additional comments in the appropriate blocks.

15. EQUIPMENT AND TRANSPORT REQUIRED (*Continued*)

17. TIME, LABOR, AND EQUIPMENT REQUIRED FOR BYPASS (*Continued*)

18. REMARKS (*Continued*)

19. ADDITIONAL COMMENTS (*Specify block.*)

Page 2, DA Form 2203-R, May 92

Enemy Demolitions Report and Enemy and/or Unidentified Minefield Report

ENEMY DEMOLITIONS REPORT

ALPHA	Map sheet(s).
BRAVO	Date and time information was collected.
CHARLIE	Location (grid coordinates) _____.
DELTA	Type of target destroyed.
ECHO	Size of the gap or area to be cleared.
FOXTROT	Possible bypass routes, time and facilities (personnel and materials) required for bypass repair or construction.
GOLF	Any other information such as local availability of construction or repair materials, material requirements, and work required, in man hours.
HOTEL	Enemy weapons or surveillance bearing on the demolition, if any.

ENEMY AND/OR UNIDENTIFIED MINEFIELD REPORT

ALPHA	Map sheet(s).
BRAVO	Date and time information was collected.
CHARLIE	Type of minefield (AT, AP, or mixed).
DELTA	Grid coordinates of minefield extremities, if known.
ECHO	Depth of minefield.
FOXTROT	Estimated time required to clear the minefield.
GOLF	
HOTEL	Estimated material and equipment required to clear the minefield.
INDIA	Routes for bypassing the minefield, if any.
JULIETT through YANKEE	Grid reference of lanes (entry and exit) and width of lanes, in meters.
ZULU	Additional information such as types of mines and fusing, description of unknown mine types, and boobytraps.

Ferry Reconnaissance Report, DA Form 1252

FERRY RECONNAISSANCE REPORT For use of this form, see FM 5-36: the proponent agency is TRADOC.	DATE
TO: *(Headquarters ordering reconnaissance)*	**FROM:** *(Name, grade and unit of reconnaissance officer)*

1. ROUTE OR LINE		2. FROM *(Initial Point)*	3. TO *(Terminal Point)*	4. DATE/TIME *(Of Signature)*
HIGHWAY	RAILROAD			

5. MAP SERIES NR	6. SHEET NUMBER	7. GRID REFERENCE		8. FERRY NR	9. CLASS
		TYPE	COORDINATES		

10. LOCATION FROM NEAREST TOWN			11. CROSSING SITE *(Name of stream or body of water)*
DISTANCE	DIRECTION	NAME OF NEAREST TOWN	

12. LIMITING FEATURE *(Condition of vessels, terminals, floods, low water, freezing, tides, etc.)* *(Seasons and Dates)*

13. WATER LEVELS *(Depths)*			14. CROSSING TIME	15. LENGTH
LOW	MEAN	HIGH		

16. VESSEL FEATURES *(Attach photographs)*

UNITS	CONSTRUC-TION TYPE	PROPULSION METHOD			LENGTH	BEAM	DRAFT	TONNAGE		CAPACITY		
		TYPE	UNITS	HP				GROSS	NET	PASS	VEHICLE	R.R. CARS

17. TERMINAL FEATURES

DIRECTION OF BANK	NAME	SLIP			DOCKING FACILITIES	APPROACHES				
		WIDTH	DEPTH	CAPACITY		HIGHWAY			RAILROAD	
						SURF	LANES	CLASS	TRACKS	SIDING
N E S W N										
N E S W N										

18. REMARKS *(Amplify above details, Note obstructions, navigational and other pertinent data)*

DA Form **1252**
1 JAN 55

Ferry Reconnaissance Report, DA Form 1252—Continued

19. ROUTE ALIGNMENT PLAN *(Indicate route, terminals, approaches, obstructions, navigational aids, direction of north arrow)*

SCALE

1 Square =

20. TERMINAL VIEWS *(Indicate slips. ramps, piling, direction of bank)*

BANK *(Circle)*

N   E   S   W   N

SCALE

1 Square =

BANK *(Circle)*

N   E   S   W   N

SCALE

1 Square =

21. REMARKS *(Attach photograph)*

Ferry Site Report and Ford Report

FERRY SITE REPORT

ALPHA	Map sheet(s).
BRAVO	Date and time information was collected.
CHARLIE	Location (grid reference or show on overlay).
DELTA	Trafficability of near and far shore routes (GO, SLOW-GO, NO GO).
ECHO	Possibilities for concealment or cover.
FOXTROT	Width of the river.
GOLF	Depth of water along ferry path and at the banks, including tidal information.
HOTEL	Stream velocity.
INDIA	Maximum slope on bank approaches and bank conditions.
JULIETT	Parking areas for road and water transport.
KILO	Any other information which could be given, such as maximum number of rafts for which site is usable, personnel hours required for preparation of approach routes, present water gauge reading (if available) and obstructions or restrictions at the site.

FORD REPORT

ALPHA	Map sheet(s).
BRAVO	Date and time information was collected.
CHARLIE	Location (grid reference or show on overlay).
DELTA	Minimum width.
ECHO	Minimum depth.
FOXTROT	Stream velocity.
GOLF	Type of bottom; for example, SOFT SANDY or FIRM ROCKY.
HOTEL	Maximum slope on banks and bank condition; for example, 9 percent - SLIPPERY CLAY.
INDIA	Trafficability of near/far shore (GO, SLOW-GO, NO GO).
JULIETT	Rise and fall of water level.
KILO	Concealment/cover.
LIMA	Any other information that could be given, such as essential limiting features or requirements for support.

Ford Reconnaissance Report, DA Form 1251

FORD RECONNAISSANCE REPORT For use of this form, see FM 5-36: the proponent agency is TRADOC.			DATE	

TO: *(Headquarters ordering reconnaissance)*		FROM: *(Name, grade and unit of reconnaissance officer)*	

I. ROUTE NUMBER	2. FROM *(Initial Point)*	3. TO *(Terminal Point)*	4. DATE/TIME *(Of signature)*

5. MAP SERIES NUMBER	6. SHEET NUMBER	7. GRID REFERENCE		8. FORD NUMBER
		TYPE	COORDINATES	

9. LOCATION FROM NEAREST TOWN			10. CROSSING *(Name of stream or other body of water)*
DISTANCE	DIRECTION	NAME OF NEAREST TOWN	

11. CHARACTERISTICS OF CROSSING

WATER LEVELS	WIDTH	DEPTH	VELOCITY	DATE	SEASON OR MONTH(S)
TODAY					
LOW					
MEAN					
HIGH					

12. BOTTOM ☐ SAND ☐ GRAVEL ☐ STONE ☐ OTHER *(Specify):*	13. APPROACHES ☐ FIRM ☐ SOFT ☐ PAVED	14. SLOPE RATIO

15. TYPE OF PAVEMENT	16. USABLE WIDTH	17. HAZARDS *(Flash floods, quicksand, etc.)*

18. REMARKS *(Description of Approach Roads, Guide Markers, Depth Gages, etc.)*

DA FORM 1251
1 JAN 55

Ford Reconnaissance Report, DA Form 1251—Continued

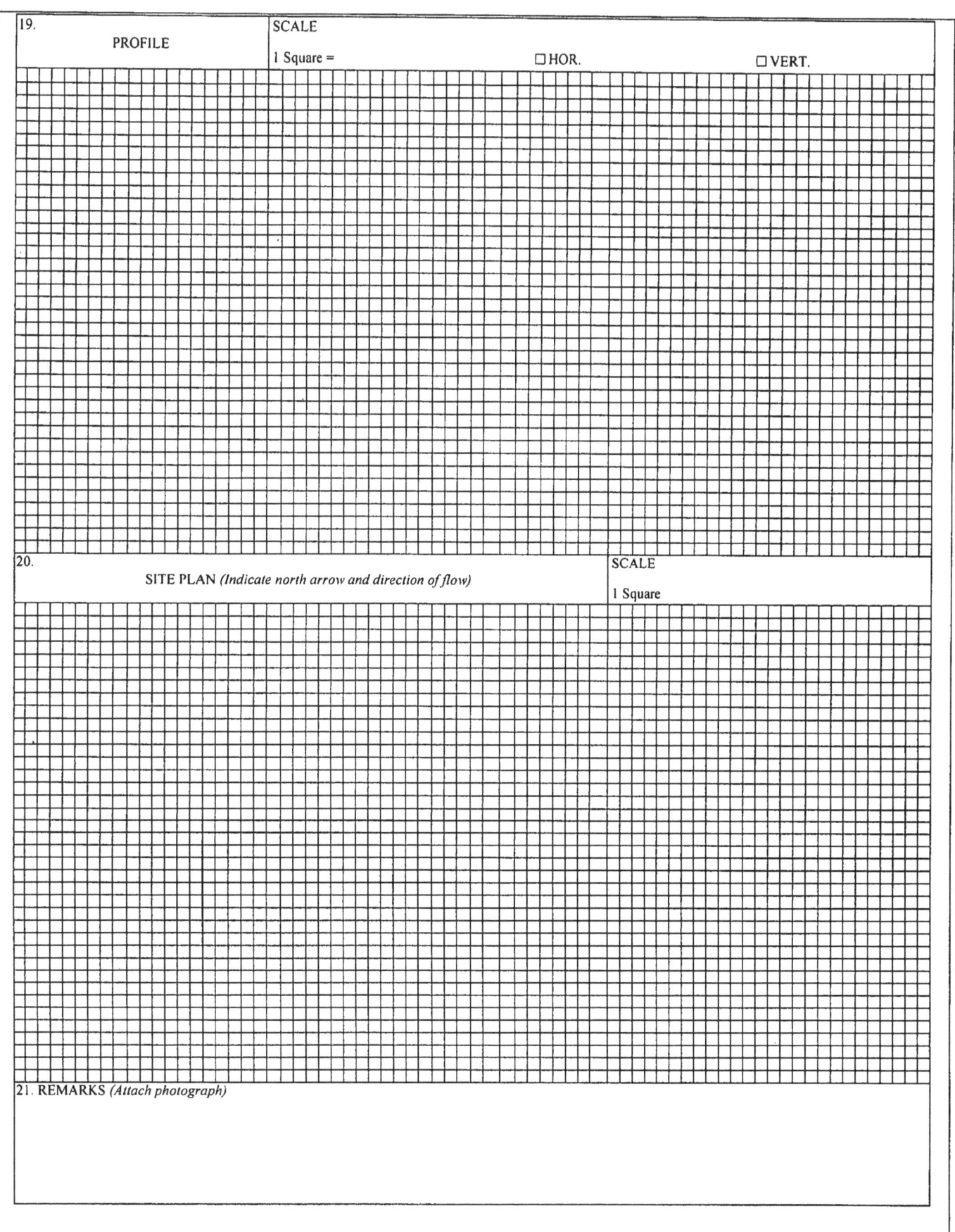

19.

PROFILE

SCALE

1 Square = ☐ HOR. ☐ VERT.

20.

SITE PLAN *(Indicate north arrow and direction of flow)*

SCALE

1 Square

21. REMARKS *(Attach photograph)*

Obstacle Report and Port Report

OBSTACLE REPORT

ALPHA	Map sheet(s).
BRAVO	Date and time information was collected.
CHARLIE	Location (grid coordinates).
DELTA	Type of obstacle.
ECHO	Enemy weapons having coverage of obstacle, if any.
FOXTROT	Any other information that could impact on breaching or bypass; for example, terrain restricts bypass, work required (in personnel hours) to breach obstacle.

PORT REPORT

ALPHA	Map sheet(s).
BRAVO	Date and time information was collected.
CHARLIE	Location (grid coordinates) .
DELTA	Environmental data. (1) Tides, (2) Winds, (3) Harbor obstructions, (4) Navigational aids, (5) Depth of main channel at low tide.
ECHO	Tug/pilot services.
FOXTROT	Berths and/or anchorages. (1) Type (concrete, stone, wood, earthen retained by seawall, etc.), (2) Length and width, (3) Single- or double-sided berthing, (4) Low tide depth at pierside, (5) Maximum load capacity.
GOLF	Pierside services. (1) Materials handling equipment (cranes, forklifts, etc.), (2) Covered and exposed warehouse space in square and cubic footage, (3) Office/administrative facilities.
HOTEL	Refueling and fuel storage facilities.
INDIA	Firefighting facilities.
JULIETT	Vehicle staging areas. (1) Size in square feet, (2) Surface material (paved, gravel, etc.), (3) Access routes, (4) Distance from berthing areas.
KILO	Access roads. (1) Classification, (2) Surface material.
LIMA	Helicopter landing areas (location[s] and capacity).
MIKE	Airfields (location[s], submit appropriate airlanding site report).
NOVEMBER	Railroad facilities and rolling stock available.
OSCAR	Additional information.

Road(s) Closed Report and Road(s) Opened Report

ROAD(S) CLOSED REPORT

ALPHA	Map sheet(s).
BRAVO	Date and time of information collection.
CHARLIE	From grid reference _____ or show on overlay.
DELTA	To grid reference_____ or show on overlay.
ECHO	Reason for closing of road (bridge destroyed at the grid reference, unusable by heavy traffic).
FOXTROT	Estimated duration.
GOLF	Detour from _____ to _____ including, if possible, class of road, or at least the following information: width of road, smooth or rough surface, gradual or sharp curves, gentle or steep grades. Classification of roads is to be given according to the weakest part of a section of road under report; that is, the class of the entire road may be restricted by a single bridge with a low military load class.
HOTEL	Cross-country bypass permitted to _____ (wheeled or tracked vehicles, and class).
INDIA	Any other information.

ROAD(S) OPENED REPORT

ALPHA	Map sheet(s).
BRAVO	Date and time the road is opened.
CHARLIE	From grid reference _____ or show on overlay.
DELTA	To grid reference_____ or show on overlay.
ECHO	Class of road and characteristics of the road to include information on shoulders. Classification of roads is given according to the weakest part or section of road under report; as an example, the class of the entire route may be by the low class of a single bridge.
FOXTROT	Minimum widths.

Road Reconnaissance Report, DA Form 1248

ROAD RECONNAISSANCE REPORT	DATE
For use of this form, see FM 5-36, proponent agency is TRADOC.	

TO (Headquarters ordering reconnaissance)	FROM: (Name, grade and unit of officer or NCO making reconnaissance)

1. MAPS	a. COUNTRY	b. SCALE	c. SHEET NUMBER OF MAPS	2. DATE/TIME GROUP (Of signature)

SECTION I - GENERAL ROAD INFORMATION

3. ROAD GRID REFERENCE		4. ROAD MARKING (Civilian or Military number of road)	5. LENGTH OF ROAD (Miles or kilometers, specify)
FROM	TO		

6. WIDTH OF ROADWAY (Feet or meters, specify)	8. WEATHER DURING RECONNAISSANCE (Include last rainfall, if known)
7. RECONNAISSANCE	
DATE TIME	

SECTION II - DETAILED ROAD INFORMATION (When circumstances permit more detailed information will be shown in an overlay or on the mileage chart on the reverse side of this form. Standard symbols will be used.)

9. ALINEMENT (Check one ONLY)	10. DRAINAGE (Check one ONLY)
(1) FLAT GRADIENTS AND EASY CURVES	(1) ADEQUATE DITCHES, CROWN/CAMBER WITH ADEQUATE CULVERTS IN GOOD CONDITION
(2) STEEP GRADIENTS (Excess of 7 in 100)	
(3) SHARP CURVES (Radius less than 100 ft [30m])	(2) INADEQUATE DITCHES, CROWN/CAMBER OR CULVERTS, ITS CULVERTS OR DITCHES ARE BLOCKED OR OTHER-WISE IN POOR CONDITION
(4) STEEP GRADIENTS AND SHARP CURVES	

11. FOUNDATION (Check one ONLY)	
(1) STABILIZED COMPACT MATERIAL OF GOOD QUALITY	(2) UNSTABLE, LOOSE OR EASILY DISPLACED MATERIAL

12. SURFACE DESCRIPTION (Complete Items 12a and b.)	
a. THE SURFACE IS (Check one ONLY)	
(1) FREE OF POTHOLES, BUMPS, OR RUTS LIKELY TO REDUCE CONVOY SPEED	(2) BUMPY, RUTTED OR POTHOLED TO AN EXTENT LIKELY TO REDUCE CONVOY SPEED
b. TYPE OF SURFACE (Check one ONLY)	
(1) CONCRETE	(6) WATERBOUND MACADAM
(2) BITUMINOUS (Specify type where known)	(7) GRAVEL
	(8) LIGHTLY METALLED
(3) BRICK (Pave)	(9) NATURAL OR STABILIZED SOIL, SAND CLAY, SHELL, CINDERS, DISINTEGRATED GRANITE, OR OTHER SELECTED MATERIAL
(4) STONE (Pave)	(10) OTHER (Describe):
(5) CRUSHED ROCK OR CORAL	

SECTION III - OBSTRUCTIONS (List in the columns below particulars of the following obstructions which affect the traffic capacity of a road. If information of any factor cannot be ascertained, insert "NOT KNOWN")
(a) Overhead obstructions, less than 14 feet or 4.25 meters, such as tunnels, bridges, overhead wires and overhanging buildings.
(b) Reductions in road widths which limit the traffic capacity, such as craters, narrow bridges, archways, and buildings.
(c) Excessive gradients (Above 7 in 100)
(d) Curves less than 100 feet (30 meters) in radius
(e) Fords

SERIAL NUMBER a	PARTICULARS b	GRID REFERENCE c	REMARKS d

DA Form **1248,**
1 JUL 60   PREVIOUS EDITION IS OBSOLETE

Road Reconnaissance Report, DA Form 1248—Continued

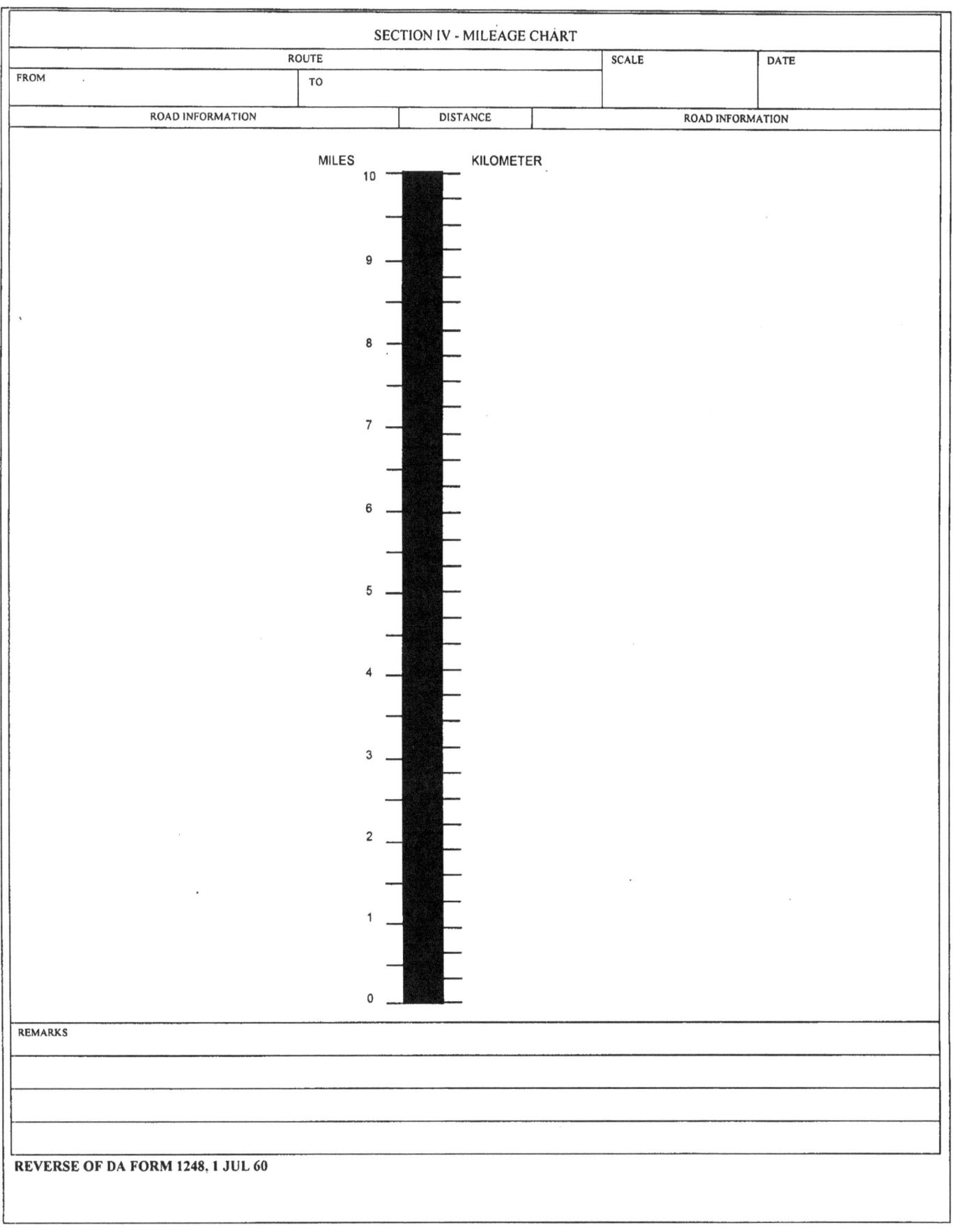

Route Closed Report and Route Opened Report

ROUTE CLOSED REPORT

ALPHA	Map sheet(s).
BRAVO	Date and time information was collected.
CHARLIE	From grid coordinates _____.
DELTA	To grid coordinates_____.
ECHO	Reason for route closure.
FOXTROT	Estimated duration.
GOLF	Detour from grid reference _____ to grid reference _____ including, if possible, military load classification of detour, widths, surface types, gradual or sharp curves, and gentle or steep grades.
HOTEL	Cross-country bypass permitted for _____ (vehicle) types and load classification number.
INDIA	Additional information.

ROUTE OPENED REPORT

ALPHA	Map sheet(s).
BRAVO	Date and time route was/will be opened.
CHARLIE	From grid coordinates _____.
DELTA	To grid coordinates_____. .
ECHO	Military load classification of route.
FOXTROT	Minimum widths.

Tunnel Reconnaissance Report, DA Form 1250

TUNNEL RECONNAISSANCE REPORT For use of this form, see FM 5-36; the proponent is TRADOC.		DATE	
TO: *(Headquarters ordering reconnaissance)*		FROM: *(Name, grade and unit of reconnaissance officer)*	

1. ROUTE OR LINE		2. FROM *(Initial Point)*	3. TO *(Terminal Point)*	4. DATE/TIME *(Of signature)*
HIGHWAY	RAILROAD			

5. MAP SERIES NR	6. SHEET NUMBER	7. GRID REFERENCE		8. TUNNEL NUMBER
		TYPE	COORDINATES	

9. LOCATION FROM NEAREST TOWN			10. TYPE *(Subaqueous, Rock, Soil)*
DISTANCE	DIRECTION	NAME OF NEAREST TOWN	

11. NAME *(Mountain or Water feature)*	12. LENGTH	13. NUMBER OF TRACKS	14. ROADWAY WIDTH

15. CLEARANCE		16. GRADE *(Percent)*	17. ALINEMENT *(Straight or radius of curve)*
VERTICAL	HORIZONTAL		

18. LINING *(Material)*	19. PORTALS *(Material)*	20. VENTILATION *(Type)*

21. DRAINAGE

22. CHAMBERED FOR DEMOLITION		23. COMPLETED *(Year)*	24. CONDITION *(Check appropriate box)*
☐ YES	☐ NO		☐ EXCELLENT ☐ GOOD ☐ FAIR ☐ POOR

25. BYPASS ABILITY

26. ALTERNATE CROSSINGS

27. APPROACHES

28. IN-TUNNEL RESTRICTIONS

29. GEOLOGICAL DATA

DA form **1250**
1 JAN 55

Tunnel Reconnaissance Report, DA Form 1250—Continued

30. PLAN AND PROFILE

PLAN SCALE
1 Square =

PROFILE SCALE
1 Square =

☐ HOR.   ☐ VERT.

31. PORTAL VIEW

SCALE
1 Square =

32. CROSS-SECTION OF BORE

SCALE
1 Square =

33. REMARKS *(Attach photograph)*

Tunnel Report

TUNNEL REPORT

ALPHA	Map sheet(s).
BRAVO	Date and time information was collected.
CHARLIE	Location (grid reference).
DELTA	Length.
ECHO	Width at most constricted diameter.
FOXTROT	Height at minimum height location.
GOLF	Gradient.
HOTEL	Type of tunnel (railroad, vehicle, footpath).
INDIA	Condition.
JULIETT	Bypass route(s) available.
KILO	Any other information that could impact on trafficability including shape of tunnel bore.

SECTION 3

COUNTERMOBILITY

Forms and Reports   · Page

Class IV and V Haul Capability

CLASS IV AND V HAUL CAPABILITY

VEHICLE	CONCERTINA WIRE	M15 MINE	M19 MINE	M21 MINE	M16 MINE	MOPMS MINE	FLIPPER MINE	VOLCANO MINE	MICLIC RELOAD
HMMWV, M998 2,500 LB 215 CU FT	2	51	34	27	55	15	11	1	*1
2 1/2 TON TRUCK 5,000 LB 443 CU FT	4	102	69	55	111	30	23	2	1
5 TON TRUCK 10,000 LB 488 CU FT	7	204	138	109	222	61	46	5	3
5 TON DUMP TRUCK 10,000 LB 135/291 CU FT ***	2/4	112/204	79/138	32/69	168/222	23/51	39/46	3/5	2/3
20 TON DUMP TRUCK 40,000 LB 754 CU FT	11	628	443	179	888	132	184	20	11
HEMITT TRUCK 20,000 LB 540 CU FT	8	408	277	128	444	94	92	10	7
12 TON S&P 24,000 LB	13	489	333	208	533	148	110	12	9
40 TON LOWBOY 80,000 LB 1,760 CU FT	27	1,466	1,035	419	1,777	308	368	43	27
M548 12,000 LB 529 CU FT	8	244	166	125	266	74	55	6	4
#MINES/ WT/LB	40/ 1,180	1/ 49	2/ 72	4/ 91	4/ 45	21/ 162	40/ 217	240/ 1,850	** 2,656
CUBE CU FT	64	1.2	1.7	4.2	0.8	5.7	3.4	37.6	64.8

#for concertina= bundles; 1 bundle = 40 rolls   *overloads vehicle   **line charge and rocket   ***without/with sideboards

Executed Demolitions Report

EXECUTED DEMOLITIONS REPORT

ALPHA	Map sheet(s).
BRAVO	Date and time of execution.
CHARLIE	Location (grid coordinates). Location and type of target destroyed should also be referred to by demolition target number or code word if any have been assigned.
DELTA	Type of target destroyed.
ECHO	Results of demolition. Size of gap, percentage of facility or material destroyed, etc.
FOXTROT	Possibility of bypassing, repairing, or restoring.
GOLF	Any other information, such as estimated effort required to repair (manhours, equipment, and material, etc.).

Field Artillery Delivered Minefield Planning Sheet, DA Form 5032-R

FIELD ARTILLERY DELIVERED MINEFIELD PLANNING SHEET
For use of this form see FM 6-20-40 or FM 6-20-50; the proponent agency is TRADOC.

SECTION A - MINEFIELD DATA

1. TARGET NUMBER	2. PRIORITY	3. REQUESTOR

4. MINEFIELD END POINTS (COORDINATES)
FROM: TO:

5. MINEFIELD DEPTH	6. MINEFIELD WIDTH
7. ADAM (APERS) DENSITY	8. RAAMS (AT) DENSITY

9. SELF-DESTRUCT TIME SHORT □ LONG □	10. SCHEDULED MINEFIELD HRS +/- MIN ON-CALL □

11. CAUTION: NLT EMPLACEMENT TIME	12. APPROVAL AUTHORITY	13. DATE-TIME GROUP (DTG)

14. REMARKS

SECTION B - G3/S3/ENGR

15. DTG RECEIVED	16. DTG SAFETY ZONE DISSEMINATED

17. REMARKS

SECTION C - FSE/FSO

18. DTG TO UNIT	19. DTG FROM UNIT	20. DTG TO G3/S3/ENGR

21. REMARKS

SECTION D - FDC DATA

22. TARGET NUMBER	23. FIRING UNIT	24. RANGE TO MINEFIELD CENTER

25. TRAJECTORY ADAM: □ HIGH □ LOW RAAMS: □ HIGH □ LOW	26. DELIVERY TECHNIQUE MET + VE/TRANSFER □ OBSERVER ADJUST □

27. AIMPOINT COORDINATE(S) (LEFT AND RIGHT OR SINGLE)

ADAM: FROM _____ TO _____   RAAMS: FROM _____ TO _____

28. DTG MISSION COMPLETED

29. REMARKS

DA Form **5032-R**

Jan 82

Conventional Minefield Requirements Computation Worksheet

CONVENTIONAL MINEFIELD REQUIREMENTS COMPUTATION WORKSHEET

GIVEN

1. Desired density   AT ___   APT ___   APB ___

2. IOE representative cluster   AT ___   APT ___   APB ___

3. Front   ___ meters

4. Depth   ___ meters

PART 1. NUMBER OF MINES.

A. Front + 9 = IOE clusters =   ___ /9 = ___ (round up)

	AT	APF	APB
B. IOE representative cluster X	___	___	___
number of IOE clusters =	x___	x___	x___
number of mines in IOE	___	___	___
C. Desired density X	___	___	___
minefield front +	x___	x___	x___
mines in regular numbered strips	___	___	___
D. Subtotal of mines (lines B + C)	___	___	___
E. 10% excess factor =	X1.10	X1.10	X1.10
Total number of mines to order	___	___	___

(round up for each)

Conventional Minefield Requirements Computation Worksheet—Continued

PART 2. NUMBER OF REGULAR LETTERED STRIPS.

A. Add desired density   AT____   +APF ____   + APB____ = ____

B. 0.6 X line A above   0.6X ___ = ___ (round up)

C. 3 X AT desired   3X ___ = ___

D. Number of regular letter strips required = highest number of lines B or C ___

PART 3. STRIP CLUSTER COMPOSITION.

A. Desired density

     AT:3X _____ = _____ APF:3X _____ = _____ APB:3X _____ = _____

B. Cluster composition table

STRIP	AT	APF	APB	STRIP TOTAL (cannot exceed 5)
A	___	___	___	___
B	___	___	___	___
C	___	___	___	___
D	___	___	___	___
E	___	___	___	___
F	___	___	___	___
G	___	___	___	___
H	___	___	___	___
COLUMN TOTAL	___	___	___	___

(cannot exceed desired density X 3 as computed in A above)

Conventional Minefield Requirements Computation Worksheet—Continued

PART 4. NUMBER OF MAN-HOURS TO INSTALL MINEFIELD.

Number of mines + emplacement rate (mines per man-hour)

Number of AT mines: ____/4 = ____ (round up)

Number APF mines: ____/8 = ____ (round up)

Number of APB mines: ____/16 = ____ (round up)

____ + ____ + ____ X 1.2 = _____ man-hours (round up)

PART 5. AMOUNT OF FENCING AND MARKING, MATERIAL

A. Concertina wire

   [(front X 2) + (depth X 2) + 160] X 1.4 = meters of concertina

   [(____ X 2) + (____ X 2) + 160] X 1.4 = (round up)

   Number of pickets = amount of concertina /15

   ____ /15 = ____ (round up)

           OR

B. Barbed wire

   [(front X 2) + (depth X 2) + 320] X 1.4 = meters of barbed wire required

   [(__ X 2) + (__ X 2) + 320] X 1.4 =__(round up)

   Number of pickets = amount of barbed wire + 30

   ____ /30 = ____ (round up)

C. Number of signs = number of pickets = _____

Conventional Minefield Requirements Computation Worksheet—Continued

PART 6. NUMBER OF TRUCKLOADS.

AT mines

_____ cases/trucks X _____ mines/case = mines/truck

_____ mines required / _____ mines/truck = _____ truckloads of AT mines

APF mines

_____ cases/trucks X _____ mines/case = _____ mines/trucks

_____ mines required / _____ mines/truck = _____ truckloads of APF mines

APB mines

_____ cases/trucks X _____ mines/case = _____ mines/trucks

_____ mines required / _____ mintes/truck = _____ truckloads of APB mines

Total truckloads

_____ AT truckloads _____ APF truckloads + _____ APB truckloads =

_____ total truckloads required (round up)

PART 7. AMOUNT OF ENGINEER TAPE..

A. Minefield
   boundaries   depth X 2 = _____ X 2 = _____

B. Regular
   lettered strips   front X number of regular strips = _____ X _____ = _____

C. IOE   front X number of IOE clusters X 3 = _____ + (_____ X 3) = _____

D. Lanes and gaps   depth X 2 X number of lanes and gaps = _____ X 2 X = _____

Conventional Minefield Requirements Computation Worksheet—Continued

E. Traffic tapes   depth X number of traffic tapes ____ X ____ = ____

F. Trip wire   front X number of regular strips with trip wire ____ X ____ = ____

    Safety tape

G. Subtotal

    A + B + C + D + E + F   ____ + ____ + ____ + ____ + ____ + ____ = ____ meters (round up)

H. Number of rolls to order

    line G X 1.2   ____ X 1.2 = ____ meters

                                  ____ meters/170 meters per roll = ____ rolls of tape (round up)

Friendly Obstacle Report and Transfer of Minefield/Obstacle

FRIENDLY OBSTACLE REPORT

ALPHA	Map sheet(s).
BRAVO	Date and time information was collected.
CHARLIE	Location (grid coordinates).
DELTA	Type of obstacle.
ECHO	Status of work.
FOXTROT	Any other information.

TRANSFER OF MINEFIELD/OBSTACLE

ALPHA	Map sheet(s).
BRAVO	Location (grid coordinates).
CHARLIE	I.D. number of obstacle.
DELTA	Transfer from (unit).
ECHO	Transfer to (unit).

SECTION 4

ENGINEER ESTIMATE, APPENDICES, AND PLANS

Forms and Reports   Page

The Engineer Estimate

(The engineer estimate is issued as a separate staff estimate.)

CLASSIFICATION

Copy ___ of ___ copies
Issuing headquarters
PLACE OF ISSUE
Date/time of issue

ENGINEER ESTIMATE NO.____

Ref: Maps, charts, or other documents.

1. MISSION

The engineer officer filling a staff position with a maneuver headquarters uses the mission statement of that headquarters in his estimate. The commander of an engineer unit supporting the maneuver headquarters performs a separate mission analysis for his unit. Therefore, a staff engineer will not perform the mission analysis steps listed under this paragraph of the estimate, but will incorporate his input into the overall staff analysis. An engineer unit commander will perform this analysis for his unit. Many times, the engineer will perform the dual role of staff engineer and engineer unit commander.

   a. Identify the Following:

      (1) Intent of the supported commander and the commander two levels up.

      (2) Area of operations.

      (3) Tasks to be performed: specified, implied, essential.

      (4) Constraints: things the supported or higher headquarters have said must be done (accomplish NLT, directed obstacles, total time available, etc.).

      (5) Restrictions: things that the supported or higher headquarters has prohibited (obstacle restricted areas).

   b. Restate the Mission. Based upon engineer's essential tasks from maneuver commander's order.

2. THE SITUATION AND COURSES OF ACTION

   a. Considerations Affecting the Possible Courses of Action

      (1) Operations to be Supported. Cover the nature of the operations, the composition of supported forces, unusual requirements, and other factors affecting the size and scope of the support mission.

(Page number)

CLASSIFICATION

The Engineer Estimate—Continued

CLASSIFICATION

(2) Characteristics of Area of Operation. Discuss the impact of the characteristics of the area of operation on the engineer's options and ability to support the operation.

    (a) Weather. Forecast weather for mission duration, ambient light data, and impact of weather on mobility, countermobility, survivability, and general engineering in the area of operations.

        1 Precipitation/temperature impact on trafficability (potential engineer missions to improve/maintain roads and trails).

        2 Precipitation impact on river crossing (depth, flow rate, bank conditions, tidal influences and ambient light availability).

        3 Precipitation/temperature impact on ability to dig (saturated/ frozen ground).

        4 Fog/limited visibility impact on positioning of obstacles.

        5 Engineer vehicle capabilities to maneuver in limited visibility vs. maneuver unit fighting vehicle capabilities.

    (b) Terrain

        1 Observation/Fields of Fire. Identify potential engineer requirements to clear fields of observation/fields of fire, special skills, equipment, and coordination necessary to clear vegetation, rubble buildings, eliminate power lines.

        2 Cover and Concealment. Consider the extent and value of existing cover and concealment such as vegetation, relief of terrain and manmade potential reinforcing obstacle locations; assess impact on requirements for survivability enhancement. Consider the protection and concealment of engineer supply points and/or equipment parks in river crossing operations.

        3 Obstacles. Identify locations and significance of existing obstacles and potential reinforcing obstacle locations. Assess impact on countermobility and/or mobility requirements for the operation.

        4 Key/Decisive Terrain. Identify key/decisive terrain in area of operation (dominant terrain, key bridges, ford sites, passes through constricted terrain). Determine potential engineer tasks required to facilitate friendly control and/or deny enemy control of this terrain.

(Page number)

CLASSIFICATION

The Engineer Estimate—Continued

CLASSIFICATION

     5 Avenues of Approach. Friendly: determine engineer requirements to support rapid movement of combat, combat support and combat service support elements along avenues of approach (reduction of existing obstacles, improving trafficability). Enemy: identify locations/engineer tasks to degrade enemy use of avenues of approach.

    (c) Other Characteristics. If pertinent, hydrography rivers, lakes and streams, transportation, telecommunications, politics, material, and personnel in area of operations that affects engineer operations.

(3) Enemy Situation. Developed in conjunction with G2/S2 analysis.

    (a) Strength, disposition, capabilities, recent and present significant activities, and likely courses of action.

    (b) Enemy capabilities affecting the mission and engineer activities. Specifically assess the availability/capabilities of enemy countermine/counterobstacle, gap crossing, and countermobility equipment and his tactics/techniques for employing it. When applicable, develop an overlay of anticipated enemy obstacles, fortifications, and other significant engineer activities.

(4) Own Situation

    (a) Tactical Situation. Examine the present dispositions of major tactical elements, possible courses of action of the supported headquarters, current operations, and projected operations.

    (b) Personnel, Logistics, and Civil Military Operations. Determine the present disposition of logistic units supporting engineer operations. Locate facilities (ASP, ATP, POL points). Determine the levels of engineer-related class IV and V items available to support the operation. Identify available indigenous support and required coordination. Assess the availability of transportation assets to support engineer operations.

    (c) Engineer Situation. Determine the present dispositions, levels of effectiveness, capabilities, and command/support relationships of engineer units. Identify combat support units that can assist with M/CM/S operations (GSRs; FA for smoke, suppression with scatterable mines; smoke generators). Examine the status of current engineer operations and establish estimated completion times. List important assumptions.

(Page number)

CLASSIFICATION

The Engineer Estimate—Continued

b. <u>Own Courses of Action</u>. Develop an engineer plan as part of each course of action being considered by the supported headquarters. The plan should attempt to create an enemy vulnerability or take advantage of an existing one.

(1) Identify requirements. Determine all tasks required for each engineer plan. Consider support needed by the maneuver forces, fire support (FA and ADA), C^3 (command posts and communication sites), CSS elements (supply routes and facilities), and that necessary due to environmental factors (support dictated by terrain, weather, NBC contamination, regardless of the maneuver scheme).

(2) Summarize resource requirements (in terms of manpower, equipment, and logistics by major supported element).

(3) Determine general priorities for tasks (based on the supported commander's guidance).

(4) Allocate engineer forces.

3. ANALYSIS OF COURSES OF ACTION

a. Wargame the engineer plan for each course of action against each anticipated enemy action/reaction. Begin with the most probable course of action. As a minimum, evaluate the plan against the significant factors that impact upon it.

b. Compare resource requirements with the assets available. Determine shortfalls.

c. Reduce the demand for engineer assets to match those available based upon time, identified shortfalls, and the enemy threat. Do this by establishing priorities, sequencing engineer activities, selecting alternate methods, and altering the engineer plan as necessary. Identify advantages and disadvantages. Engineer support to critical maneuver events must be forthcoming. If the engineer plan cannot meet the minimum maneuver requirements, then it is not feasible and the plan under consideration ceases to be valid.

4. COMPARISON OF COURSES OF ACTION

The engineer on a maneuver headquarters staff selects the best course of action from an engineer perspective. That recommendation is then provided to the maneuver G3/S3 for incorporation into his decision process for the maneuver commander. The engineer recommendation is usually summarized as one factor among others for the commander to consider.

The supporting engineer commander or his staff chooses the course of action that will best accomplish the engineer unit's mission.

The Engineer Estimate—Continued

CLASSIFICATION

The decision may be quantified by using a comparison/decision matrix, which is developed in the same manner by either the engineer staff officer or commander. The significant factors, upon which the decision will be based, are selected and listed. The ability of each course of action to meet the requirements of each significant factor is assessed. A subjective judgment then determines the best course of action.

5. RECOMMENDATION/DECISION

The engineer staff officer makes his recommendation to the supported commander.

The recommendation begins with a statement as to the supportability of the maneuver course of action under consideration. (If the maneuver scheme's success depends on engineer support, and a proposed course of action could not be supported by engineers, that should have already been resolved prior to this step by eliminating the entire proposed course of action.) State which course of action can best be supported from the engineer perspective.

Cover major deficiencies from the engineer perspective. Include recommendations for eliminating or reducing them.

Recommend task organizations, command/support relationships, obstacles/tasks to be directed to subordinate elements, and priorities of effort.

_____

(Engineer officer)

Annexes: (as required)

(Page number)

CLASSIFICATION

Engineer Appendix to the Combat Service Support Annex

This is a sample engineer appendix to a combat service support annex. Though not included in this sample, the scope of the operation involved may dictate the inclusion of tabs addressing the concept of engineer operations such as major engineer tasks, unit assignments and priorities, road and bridge plans and criteria, airfield development, and control of class IV material.

CLASSIFICATION

Copy ___ of ___ copies
Issuing headquarters
PLACE OF ISSUE
Date/time of issue

APPENDIX____(Engineer) to ANNEX P (Combat Service Support) to Operation Plan_____

Ref: (a) Maps: Sheet, Series, Scale
     (b) Etc.

Time Zone: X

Task Organization: See Annex A (Task Organization) to Operation Plan_____

1. SITUATION

   a. Enemy Forces. See Annex B (Intelligence) to Operation Plan_____

   b. Friendly Forces. See Operation Plan_____ and Appendix I (Operation Overlay) to Annex C (Operations) of the OPLAN.

2. MISSION

   Landing force engineer group (XXXX) supports landing force (XXXX); supports the forward movement of the landing force; provides construction, rehabilitation, and maintenance of airfield facilities; prepares to rehabilitate ports; and performs engineer tasks in the area as required.

3. EXECUTION

   a. Commander's Intent and Concept of Operations.

      (1) Commander's Intent (Optional).

      (2) Concept of Engineer Operations. See Tab ____ (Concept of Engineer Operations).

(Page number)

CLASSIFICATION

Engineer Appendix to the Combat Service Support Annex—Continued

CLASSIFICATION

    b. Landing Force Engineer Group

       (1) On order, lands over designated beaches and/or ports and provides general engineer support to the task force.

       (2) Provide construction, rehabilitation, and maintenance of airfield facilities.

       (3) Be prepared to commence rehabilitation and maintenance of ports on order.

       (4) Assume assigned construction projects and priorities.

    c. Coordinating Instructions

       (1) Upon establishment ashore of the landing force engineer group, routine engineer support will be provided to the landing force on a mission basis; missions to be designated.

       (2) Command of landing force engineer group will pass to commanding officer 8th ESBn in the event that the landing force engineer becomes a casualty.

       (3) Roads and Bridges

          (a) Initial development of roads, other than those of a combat support type, will be based on the master roads priorities as established by Tab_____(Major Engineer Tasks, Unit Assignments, and Priorities) and Tab_____(Road and Bridge Plan).

          (b) Use of organic bridging will be made only on order of TF ____.

       (4) Mines and Unexploded Ordnance

          (a) Mines and unexploded ordnance will be removed in the following order of priority:

             1 Area for the advance of the assault elements.

             2 Airfields and sites for airfields.

             3 Routes of communication.

             4 Combat service support organizations.

             5 Command post areas.

             6 Civilian areas.

(Page number)

CLASSIFICATION

Engineer Appendix to the Combat Service Support Annex—Continued

(b) Hasty protective minefields installed for temporary local defense may be authorized by commanders. Such minefields will always be removed by the unit authorizing emplacement unless otherwise directed.

(c) Minefields, other than hasty protective, will not be placed in MEF areas of responsibility without approval of the MEF commander, or those subordinate commanders to which the MEF commander has delegated approval authority. When command is passed ashore, minefield authority will pass also.

(d) Reports and records of all minefields will be in accordance with FM 20-32 and II MEF Order ____.

(5) <u>Demolitions</u>

(a) Major installations and facilities will be prepared for demolition. Demolitions will not be placed, but will be kept available so that they may be rapidly employed when ordered.

(b) Installations and facilities to be prepared for demolitions include the following:

<u>1</u> Bridges.

<u>2</u> Cut and fill sections on major routes.

<u>3</u> Airfields.

<u>4</u> Railroads.

<u>5</u> CSS installations.

<u>6</u> Utilities and water supply installations.

(6) <u>Water Supply</u>

(a) Commanders will embark sufficient water supply equipment to provide water for all units in their respective areas.

(b) Emphasis will be placed on the location of fresh water sources so that field purification equipment may be used.

(c) Existing water supply facilities will be rehabilitated and expanded as soon as possible, and as determined by the landing force engineer.

Engineer Appendix to the Combat Service Support Annex—Continued

CLASSIFICATION

(7) Airfield development will be of a temporary nature, but design and location will be planned to facilitate future development. Existing airfields will be developed, repaired, and maintained in accordance with Tab ___ (Airfield Development).

(8) Building construction for billeting of personnel will be of the most temporary nature.

(9) Port rehabilitation and construction will be of a temporary nature.

(10) Railroads, rolling stock, and locomotives will be reported to the MEF commander.

(11) Deception and camouflage of vehicles and installations will be maximized.

(12) Bulk fuel will be under the control of LFSP initially; commander, 2d FSSG on order. Engineer support will be provided as required. See Appendix ____ (Bulk Fuel) to Annex P (Combat Service Support) to Operation Plan_____.

(13) Mapping and survey priorities will be determined by the MEF commander. Landing force engineer will direct third order ground control survey and any extensions thereof.

(14) Indigenous labor will be used to the greatest extent possible. See Annex ____ (Civil Affairs) to Operation Plan_____.

(15) All local construction materials uncovered will be reported to the task force commander for control and release.

(16) Reports: All reports will be submitted IAW II MEF Order ____.

4. ADMINISTRATION AND LOGISTICS

a. Class IV engineer materials listed in Tab ____ will be embarked by 2d FSSG and will be controlled by the MEF commander.

b. Major class II engineer items to be embarked will be reported for prior approval.

5. COMMAND AND SIGNAL

a. See Annex K (Communications-Electronics) to Operation Plan _____.

(Page number)

CLASSIFICATION

Engineer Appendix to the Combat Service Support Annex—Continued

CLASSIFICATION

    b. Command Posts

       (1) Afloat-Aboard (ship hull #).

       (2) Ashore-TBD.

ACKNOWLEDGE RECEIPT

               BY COMMAND OF _____

                       Signature
                   Grade   Service
                       Billet

TABS:

    A - Concept of Engineer Operations
    B - Major Engineer Tasks, Unit Assignments, and Priorities
    C - Road and Bridge Plan
    D - Airfield Development
    E - Controlled Class IV Engineer Items

DISTRIBUTION: See Annex _____ (Distribution) to Operation Plan _____.

(Page number)

CLASSIFICATION

Engineer Appendix to an Operation Order

CLASSIFICATION

Copy no ___ of ___ copies
Issuing Headquarters
PLACE OF ISSUE
Date/time of issue

APPENDIX ____(Engineer) to ANNEX C (Operations) to Operation Plan_____

Ref: (a) Maps: Sheet, Series, Scale
      (b) Engineer Operations SOP

Time Zone: X

Task Organization: See Annex A (Task Organization) to Operation Plan_____

1. SITUATION

    a. Enemy Forces. See Annex B (Intelligence) to Operation Plan_____.

    b. Friendly Forces. See Operation Plan_____.

    c. Attachments and Detachments

        (1) Co. A, 8th ESBn attached effective DTG.

        (2) 1st Plt Bridge Co., 8th ESBn reinforces Co. A, 8th ESBn.

    d. Assumptions. That surf conditions will allow the landing of heavy engineer equipment and material on D-day.

2. MISSION

2d Marine Division (rein), commencing at H-hour on D-day, conducts a surface assault over beach #4 of Cyprus; commencing at L-hour on D-day, conducts a helicopterborne assault of objective H; seizes objectives A through J in order to seize the port of Famagusta communication center at Nicosia; prepares to continue the attack and seize the remainder of the island on order.

(Page number)

CLASSIFICATION

Engineer Appendix to an Operation Order—Continued

CLASSIFICATION

3. EXECUTION

    a. Commander's Intent and Concept of Operations.

        (1) Commander's Intent (Optional).

        (2) Concept of Operations

            (a) Reinforced combat engineer companies are attached to the surface assault regimental landing teams (RLT) to provide close combat engineer support in the respective RLT zones of action. A combat engineer company (-) is attached to the helicopter and assault RLT to provide close combat engineer support for that unit. Attached combat engineer companies will revert to control of 2d CEBn on order. The 2d CEBn (-) (Rein) will land over beach #4 on D-day prepared to provide close combat engineer support to the division as required. Elements of one engineer company from 8th ESBn, with adequate bridging assets, will land over beach #4 on D-day. The remainder of that company and the remaining bridge assets will land at Famagusta commencing late D + 1. Attached companies will revert to parent control on order.

            (b) Maximum effort will be made to complete installation of bridges over Tremithos River on D-day. Highest priority assigned to engineer tasks relating to repair of critical routes of communication.

            (c) Clearance of enemy emplaced obstacles will be a continuing requirement.

    b. RLT2

        (1) Conduct breaching operations in accordance with Appendix ____ (Breaching Plan) to Annex C (Operations) to Operation Plan _____.

        (2) Within capabilities, repair and reinforce bridges at _____ and _____ if required. If bridges are beyond repair, commence preparation of crossing site until relieved by 2d CEBn (-) (Rein).

    c. RLT6

        (1) Conduct breaching operations in accordance with Appendix ____ (Breaching Plan) to Annex C (Operations) to Operation Plan _____.

        (2) Within capabilities, clear mines from and initiate repairs to MSR from Blue Beach to Larnaca.

        (3) Within capabilities, initiate repair and reinforce bridge at _____ if required.

    d. RLT8 Within capabilities, initiate repair of main runways at Nicosia airfield.

(Page number)

CLASSIFICATION

Engineer Appendix to an Operation Order—Continued

CLASSIFICATION

e. 2d CEBn (-) (Rein)

(1) Land on order and support the assault.

(2) Repair, install, maintain, and operate bridging at coordinates and if required. Specific sites to be determined by reconnaissance.

(3) Provide close combat engineer support to the division, as required.

(4) Be prepared on order to assume missions assigned to engineer elements in support of RLTs 2 and 6.

(5) On order, resume control of detached elements of the battalion.

(6) Be prepared to repair and maintain the airfield at Nicosia to accept air traffic by D+5.

(7) Develop and maintain routes of communication in the zone of action.

f. Coordinating Instructions

(1) Mines and Obstacles

(a) Breaching and mine clearance operations: reference (b) and Appendix ____ (Breaching Plan) to Annex C (Operations) to Operation Plan _____.

(b) Priority of clearance of mines and obstacles:

1 Those limiting tactical operations.

2 Those limiting combat service support operations.

(c) Employment of mines and obstacles:

1 Emplacement IAW reference ____.

2 Reporting and recording IAW FM 20-32.

3 All minefield emplacement, except hasty protective minefields, requires approval of BLT commander or above.

(2) Demolitions. Be prepared to conduct demolition of following types of installations on order: bridges, airfields, and CSS installations.

(3) Roads and Bridges

(a) Priority of maintenance and repair to MSRs.

(b) Provide fragmentary reports of capacity and condition of uncovered bridges by most rapid means to this headquarters.

(Page number)
CLASSIFICATION

Engineer Appendix to an Operation Order—Continued

CLASSIFICATION

    (4) <u>Engineer Assistance</u>. Provide equipment and technical assistance for tactical requirements to include:

        (a) Deception operations.

        (b) Artillery and other weapons positions.

        (c) Helicopter landing sites.

    (5) <u>Engineer Reconnaissance</u>

        (a) IAW reference ____.

        (b) Highest priority to reconnaissance information requested in Annex B (Intelligence) to Operation Plan ____.

    (6) <u>Reports</u>. Submit IAW Appendix ____ (Reports) to Annex P (Combat Service Support) to Operation Plan ____ .

4. ADMINISTRATION AND LOGISTICS

  a. <u>Classes I-IX Supplies Available</u>. See Annex P (Combat Service Support) to Operation Plan ____.

  b. <u>Class IV Engineer Items Available</u>

    (1) <u>Fortification Material</u>

        (a) Each vehicle 1quarter-ton and larger.

            <u>1</u> 2 rolls concertina on front bumper.

            <u>2</u> 4 bundles sandbags in cargo space.

        (b) 2d CEBn (-)(Rein) loads organic vehicles with barbed wire and pickets for minefield marking.

        (c) Landing Force Support Party (LFSP).

            <u>1</u> 5 rolls concertina.

            <u>2</u> 500 long pickets.

            <u>3</u> 4 bags of staples.

            <u>4</u> 500,000 sandbags.

    (2) <u>Construction Material</u>

(Page number)

CLASSIFICATION

Engineer Appendix to an Operation Order—Continued

CLASSIFICATION

       (a) <u>2d CEBn (-) (Rein).</u> See Appendix ____ (Civil Engineer Support Plan) to Annex D (Logistics) to Operations Plan ____.

       (b) <u>2d FSSG</u>

           <u>1</u> 50,000 BF lumber (various sizes).

           <u>2</u> 1000# nails (various sizes).

     c. <u>Distribution of Engineer Items</u>

       (1) Engineer supplies initially drawn from LFSP.

       (2) Control of issue: see reference (__).

5. <u>COMMAND AND SIGNAL</u>

     a. <u>See Annex K</u>. (Communications-Electronics) to Operation Plan ____.

     b. <u>Command Posts</u>

       (1) Afloat: (ship hull designator), 2d CEBn (-) (Rein).

       (2) Ashore: 2d CEBn: Report when established.

ACKNOWLEDGE RECEIPT

               BY COMMAND OF _____

                          Signature
                       Grade   Service
                           Billet

<u>DISTRIBUTION</u>: See Annex Z (Distribution)

(Page number)

CLASSIFICATION

Breaching Plan Appendix

The breaching plan is normally appendix 15 to the operations annex.

CLASSIFICATION

> Copy ___ of ___ copies
> Issuing headquarters
> PLACE OF ISSUE
> Date/time of issue

APPENDIX___(Breaching Plan) to ANNEX C (Operations) to Operation Plan ___

Ref: (a) SOP for Breaching Operations
(b) FMFM 13-7, *MAGTF Breaching Operations*

Time Zone: X

1. SITUATION

   a. Enemy Forces. Refer to Annex B (Intelligence) and current INTSUM. Describe enemy obstacle capability and probability of employment.

   b. Friendly Forces. Note higher, adjacent, and supporting forces involved in the operation.

   c. Attachments and Detachments. Refer to Annex A (Task Organization): support, assault, and breach force organization.

   d. Assumptions. State any assumptions on which obstacle breaching planning is based.

2. MISSION

   State the mission to be accomplished by obstacle breaching operations.

3. EXECUTION

   a. Commander's Intent and Concept of Operations.

      (1) Commander's Intent (Optional).

      (2) Concept of Operations. Summarize the intended course of action for obstacle breaching operations.

   b. Tasks. In separate numbered paragraphs, assign breaching tasks and responsibilities to each appropriate unit.

   c. Coordinating Instructions. Include coordination and control measures applicable to two or more units. The marking system should be well defined to include the location of traffic control guides and traffic priority.

(Page number)

CLASSIFICATION

Breaching Plan Appendix—Continued

CLASSIFICATION

4. ADMINISTRATION AND LOGISTICS

Refer to Annex P (Combat Service Support). Provide a statement of the combat service support requirements for obstacle breaching operations, including re-supply.

5. COMMAND AND SIGNAL

Refer to Annex K (Communications-Electronics) and include any special instructions such as use of smoke.

/S/ _____
————————————

(Page number)

CLASSIFICATION

Obstacle Plan Appendix

Obstacle plans are normally prepared at MEB/MEU level.

CLASSIFICATION

Copy ___ of ___ copies
Issuing headquarters
PLACE OF ISSUE
Date/time of issue

APPENDIX_____(Obstacle Plan) to ANNEX C (Operations) to Operation Order_____.

Ref: (a) Maps: Sheet, Series, Scale

Time Zone: X

1. SITUATION

    a. Enemy Forces. Refer to Annex B (Intelligence) and current INTSUM.

    b. Friendly Forces. Note higher, adjacent, and supporting forces involved in the operation.

    c. Attachments and Detachments. Refer to Annex A (Task Organization).

    d. Assumptions. State any assumption upon which obstacle planning is based.

2. MISSION. State the desired obstacle effect on the enemy to be accomplished by employment of obstacles; i.e., block, turn, fix, disrupt.

3. EXECUTION

    a. Commander's Intent and Concept of Operations.

        (1) Commander's Intent (Optional).

        (2) Concept of Operations. Summarize the intended course of action for obstacle employment. The concept indicates the general trace of assigned zones and obstacle restricted areas, as well as gaps and lanes. It also specifies the priority in which construction effort will be applied to each zone.

    b. Tasks. In separate numbered subparagraphs, assign tasks or responsibilities to each appropriate unit. Obstacle zone construction responsibilities are assigned in this paragraph.

(Page number)

CLASSIFICATION

Obstacle Plan Appendix—Continued

Example:

Obstacle Zone Construction Responsibilities:

(1) 9th Marines (Security Force)

ZONE(S)	PRIORITY	REMARKS
BILL	1	Disruption belts in assigned zones.
JOHN	2	

(2) 3d Marines (Left Sector)

ZONE(S)	PRIORITY	REMARKS
GEORGE	3	Site fixing belts to support kill zone.
PHIL	4	Note location of gaps through zone.
TONY	5	Note location of gaps through zone.
TIM	7	

Submit plans for closing gaps in TONY and PHIL to this HQ ASAP.

(3) 4th Marines (Right Sector)

ZONE(S)	PRIORITY	REMARKS
DAVID	6	Site belts to best conform to your scheme of maneuver.
BOB	8	

(4) 3d Combat Engineer Battalion. Assist regiments with obstacle construction in accordance with this order. Priority of effort to 3d Marines.

c. Coordinating Instructions. Include coordination and control measures applicable to two or more units.

Example:

(1) Submit belt location overlay to this HQ NLT _____.

(2) Construction of obstacles will begin immediately.

(3) Only protective obstacles will be constructed outside of assigned zones.

(4) In the event combat engineer companies are attached to regiments for assisting with spoiling and counterattacks, attachments from 9th ESBn will remain in direct support of the division to continue work on obstacle construction.

(5) Request authority from this HQ for changes to zone boundaries as well as for additional gaps and lanes.

(Page number)

Obstacle Plan Appendix—Continued

CLASSIFICATION

(6) Toxic chemicals (except napalm) not authorized.

(7) Designated firing teams will be at all reserved demolition targets at all times when demolitions are in place.

(8) Improvement of obstacle system will continue during occupancy of the battle area.

(9) Report change of status of targets to division immediately.

(10) All bridge targets will be dual-primed electrically with backup nonelectric charge planned.

(11) All crater targets will be dual-primed nonelectrically with backup electric caps available.

(12) Exploit civilian labor to maximum. Labor force transportation will be coordinated by the engineer officer. See details on use of civilians in Annex D (Logistics) and Annex P (Combat Service Support).

4. ADMINISTRATION AND LOGISTICS. Refer to Annex P (Combat Service Support). Provide a statement of the combat service support requirements for employment of obstacles.

5. COMMAND AND SIGNAL. Refer to Annex K (Communications-Electronics) and include any special instructions.

a. Ensure that all appropriate minefield and obstacle reports are submitted up the chain of command.

b. Include any restrictions on use of mines and authorization required to emplace various types of minefields.

c. Close gaps and lanes, destroy bridges, and blow craters on division order or as tactical situation dictates.

ACKNOWLEDGE RECEIPT

BY COMMAND OF _____

Signature
Grade   Service
Billet

DISTRIBUTION: See Annex Z (Distribution)

(Page number)

CLASSIFICATION

Bulk Fuel Plan

CLASSIFICATION

Copy no. ___ of ___ copies
Issuing headquarters
PLACE OF ISSUE
Date/time of issue

TAB_____to APPENDIX (Supply) to ANNEX_____(Combat Service Support) to
Operation Order_____.

Ref: (a) Maps: Sheet, Series, Scale,

Time Zone: X

1. SITUATION

    a. Enemy Forces. See Annex B (Intelligence) to Operation Plan_____.

    b. Friendly Forces. See Annex A (Task Organization) to Operation Plan _____.

    c. Assumptions. Requirements and premise used as a basis for the plan.

2. MISSION

Perform all functions incident to the supply of bulk class III and III (A) to elements ashore. Utilize existing fuel storage resources if possible, particularly in the
vicinities of coordinates (_____) and (_____).

3. EXECUTION

    a. Commander's Intent and Concept of Operations.

        (1) Commander's Intent (Optional).

        (2) Concept of Operations. See Tab A to this appendix.

    b. Landing Force Support Party

Example:

    (1) Land on order over Green Beach with one AAFS.

    (2) Establish fuel farm in wooded area on left flank of GREEN ONE. Be pre-
        pared to tie in with the 6-inch ship-to-shore bulk fuel delivery system by
        D+2.

    (3) Disperse fuel farm as fire protection against enemy action.

    (4) Report exact location and time of opening by most rapid means to this
        headquarters.

    (5) Provide three refuelers for fuel delivery until support units land.

(Page number)
CLASSIFICATION

Bulk Fuel Plan—Continued

CLASSIFICATION

c. 2d Marine Division

Example:

    (1) Land with all vehicles fully fueled.

    (2) Utilize point distribution to maximum extent possible; emergency delivery available upon request using LFSP tanker trucks.

d. 2d Force Service Support Group

Example:

    (1) Land with two AAFS.

    (2) Be prepared to assume on order control of the fuel farm on beach GREEN ONE.

    (3) Be prepared to transfer and store fuel for wing units at coordinates _____ and _____.

    (4) Locate AAFS in vicinity coordinates to support helicopter and V/STOL aircraft operations.

    (5) Report location of fuel transfer lines, fuel farms, and time and dates of opening by most expedient means to this headquarters.

    (6) Provide refuelers for fuel delivery as required.

e. 2d Marine Air Wing

Example:

    (1) Be prepared to receive, store, and issue bulk fuel at the designated airfield from 2d FSSG.

    (2) Provide refueler trucks for transfer of fuel and backup fuel stocks to bulk fuel system.

    (3) Be prepared to provide two HERS systems for resupply of helicopters at two remote sites.

f. Coordinating Instructions

Example:

    (1) 2d FSSG responsible for internal security of fuel sites other than at airfields. Coordination with local commanders required.

(Page number)

CLASSIFICATION

Bulk Fuel Plan—Continued

CLASSIFICATION

(2) Dispersion and camouflage consistent with enemy threat emphasized.

(3) Submit reports IAW Annex_____(Reports).

4. ADMINISTRATION AND LOGISTICS

a. See Annex P (Combat Service Support) to Operation Plan_____.

b. Identify Command Posts.

(1) Afloat: TBD.

(2) Ashore: Report location to LFSP and this headquarters by most expedient means.

5. COMMAND AND SIGNAL

See Annex K (Communications-Electronics) to Operation Plan_____.

ACKNOWLEDGE RECEIPT

BY COMMAND OF _____

Signature
Grade   Service
Billet

DISTRIBUTION: See Annex Z (Distribution) to Operations Plan _____.

(Page number)

CLASSIFICATION

Civil Engineer Support Plan

Copy no. ___ of ___copies
Issuing Headquarters
PLACE OF ISSUE
Date/time of issue

APPENDIX 5 (Civil Engineering Support Plan) to ANNEX D (Logistics) to
CINCLANTFLT Operation Plan_____.

Ref: (a) Maps: Sheet, Series, Scale
  (b) SOPs
  (c) Etc.

Time Zone: X

1. GENERAL

  a. Purpose. A statement of the broad purpose of the CESP.

  b. Scope/Limitations. A statement of the general character and magnitude of the
    civil engineering requirements in the area of operations. Includes gross esti-
    mates of the anticipated enemy damage and any constraints affecting the
    CESP.

  c. Engineering Intelligence

    (1) Refers to Annex B (Intelligence) for significant intelligence concerning
      climate, terrain, hydrography, and natural and industrial resources in the
      area of operations.

    (2) Lists sources of engineer intelligence data, including dates of information.

  d. Definitions. Lists definitions which are necessary to understand this plan but
    are not in the Joint dictionary of terms or the glossary of the parent operation
    order.

  e. International Agreements and Political Factors

    (1) General. Summarizes agreements, other arrangements, and political factors
      affecting the CESP.

    (2) Real Property: States the local policies for real property acquisition and
      use.

    (3) Host Nation Support. Discusses use of the following:

      (a) Indigenous labor.

(Page number)

Civil Engineer Support Plan—Continued

CLASSIFICATION

    (b) Availability of local construction materials, supplies, and equipment.

    (c) Third-country labor force.

    (d) Local contractors.

    (e) Local facilities.

  (4) Limiting Factors. Identifies rights, agreements, or other arrangements not now in existence that will be required to execute the plan.

f. Construction Standards. Indicates the construction standards as outlined in chapter 6, volume I, Joint Pub 3-0, to be used by all Service components in the operational area and explains proposed deviations from these established standards.

g. Planning Factors. Explains proposed deviations from the joint planning factors for military construction in contingency operations.

h. General Priority of Development. Explains the concept of the CESP in sufficient detail for analysis. Includes areas such as geographic, functional, and base priorities; theater construction policy; etc.

i. Protective Construction Policy. Defines the command policy for protective construction and repair of damage. Discusses general policy including:

  (1) Statement of the enemy's capability to inflict damage.

  (2) Protection required for weapons systems, personnel, and material.

  (3) Self-help vs. engineer troop effort.

j. Contractors. Discusses the availability and possible use of U.S. or third country construction contractors.

2. RESPONSIBILITIES FOR CIVIL ENGINEERING SUPPORT PLANNING

a. Primary Responsibility. Identifies each echelon of joint command having responsibility for civil engineering support planning; e.g., combined, subordinate, unified, or joint task force, and identifies specific tasks of each.

b. Supporting Responsibility. Identifies civil engineering support planning responsibilities of each Service component command to the operation plan. LOCs and bases (e.g., ports, depots, and airfields) may be jointly used and will require designation of one component commander with responsibility to ensure complete integrated planning, subsequent programming, and necessary coordination and construction.

(Page number)

CLASSIFICATION

Civil Engineer Support Plan—Continued

CLASSIFICATION

3. COMMAND RELATIONSHIPS

Indicates recommendations, if any, to deviate from existing command relationships as they relate to the execution of the construction programs described in this appendix.

4. TIME-PHASED REQUIREMENTS LISTS

From the information in the CESP, summarize the required and expected phasing of facilities, war damage repair, engineering of construction forces, and construction materials. When submitted with the operation plan, a tape of dependent files, parameters, and output products must be submitted to the Director of Logistics for the Joint Staff. This paragraph must include a statement that the submission has been made.

5. SUMMARY OF CRITICAL FACTORS AFFECTING THE CESP

This paragraph is analytical and is oriented toward the major problem areas in the CESP that may inhibit operation plan implementation until they are resolved. Possible solutions to these problem areas should be analyzed and the implications of each alternative should be evaluated in terms of its impact on the operation plan.

ACKNOWLEDGE RECEIPT

BY COMMAND OF _____

Signature
Grade   Service
Billet

DISTRIBUTION: See Annex Z (Distribution) to Operations Plan _____.

TAB(s) (If required.)

(Page number)

CLASSIFICATION

Engineer Barrier Plan

Barrier plans are strategic, not tactical in nature, and are prepared at MEF or higher level headquarters.

CLASSIFICATION

Copy no ___ of ___ copies
Issuing Headquarters
PLACE OF ISSUE
Date/time of issue

APPENDIX___ (Barrier) to ANNEX C (Operations) to Operation Plan___

Ref: (a) Maps: Sheet, Series, Scale,
(b) SOP for Engineer Operations

Time Zone: X

1. SITUATION

a. Enemy Forces. See Annex B (Intelligence) to Operation Plan_____.

b. Friendly Forces

(1) See Operation Plan No. _____.

(2) 8th Engineer Support Battalion (-), Direct Support, 2d Marine Division.

(3) 30th Naval Construction Brigade, General Support, 2d Marine Division.

c. Assumptions

(1) All streams generally are fordable, but only with difficulty.

(2) A labor of approximately 500 civilians will be available to assist in the construction of the barrier system.

2. MISSION

Prepare barrier system to impede enemy maneuver in assigned sector, deny terrain to the enemy, and stop enemy in zone.

3. EXECUTION

a. Commander's Intent and Concept of Operations.

(1) Commander's Intent (Optional).

(2) Concept of Operations

(a) MEF employs obstacles to facilitate accomplishment of assigned mission.

(b) The obstacle zones and friendly defensive works are designed to disorganize, deceive, and delay the enemy.

(Page number)
CLASSIFICATION

Engineer Barrier Plan—Continued

CLASSIFICATION

(c) Tab A (MEF Barrier Location Concept) indicates the general trace of the MEF barrier including minefields, gaps, lanes, and other manmade/ reinforced natural obstacles. Unless otherwise specified, obstacle zones will be constructed in the following order of priority:

1 Covering obstacle zone.

2 Forward obstacle zone.

3 Intermediate obstacle zone.

(d) Flank and rear area security obstacle systems will be constructed by designated II MEF forces.

b. 2d Marines

OBSTACLE/TGT	COORD	PRI	REMARKS
D-E-F			Forward obstacle zone
1-XX-31MF	XXXXXX	1	8th ESBn will site, mark,
1-XX-32MF	XXXXXX	2	and record minefields.
1-XX-34MF	XXXXXX	3	
E-J		4	Intermediate obstacle zone

c. 6th Marines

OBSTACLE/TGT	COORD	PRI	REMARKS
F-G-H			Forward obstacle zone
1-XX-35MF	XXXXXX	1	8th ESBn will site, mark,
1-XX-36MF	XXXXXX	2	and record minefields.
1-XX-39MF	XXXXXX	3	
1-XX-42MF	XXXXXX	4	
F-K			Intermediate obstacle zone
G-L			Intermediate obstacle zone

d. 2d Combat Engineer Bn

OBSTACLE/TGT	COORD	PRI	REMARKS
A-B		1	integrate existing obstacle targets I-29 into overall co-ordinating barrier plan.
E-J		2	Assist 2d Marines.
F-K		3	Assist 6th Marines.

(Page number)

CLASSIFICATION

Engineer Barrier Plan—Continued

G-L		4	Assist 6th Marines.
1-XX-80MF	XXXXXX	5	Coordinating w/division reserve.

e. Coordinating Instructions

    (1) 30th NCB general support of 2d MarDiv. Intended support is the installation of 27 flank and rear area mobility/countermobility projects (e.g., tank ditches, nonexplosive obstacle installation).

    (2) 8th ESBn direct support of 2d MarDiv. Intended primary support is installation of minefields along FEBA as listed below and LOC maintenance:

OBSTACLE/TGT	COORD	PRI	REMARKS
1-XX-31MF	XXXXXX	1	Make liaison w/2d Marines.
1-XX-32MF	XXXXXX	2	Make liaison w/2d Marines.
1-XX-34MF	XXXXXX	3	Make liaison w/2d Marines.
1-XX-35MF	XXXXXX	4	Make liaison w/6th Marines.
1-XX-36MF	XXXXXX	5	Make liaison w/6th Marines.
1-XX-39MF	XXXXXX	6	Make liaison w/6th Marines.
1-XX-42MF	XXXXXX	7	Make liaison w/6th Marines.

    (3) Request authority for additional lanes and gaps.

    (4) Close gaps and lanes on division order.

    (5) Toxic chemicals (except napalm) not authorized.

    (6) After withdrawal of GOP, GOP commander executes barrier targets within security area.

    (7) Once divisional targets are prepared for demolition, a firing team will remain on site unti target execution or until properly relieved.

    (8) Barrier construction will begin on order and improvements will be continuous.

    (9) Report target status changes to division immediately.

    (10) Complete barrier plan must remain at divisional level; extracts authorized at forward regiment CP level.

(Page number)

Engineer Barrier Plan—Continued

CLASSIFICATION

    (11) Bridge targets will be dual-primed electrically.

    (12) Crater targets will be dual-primed nonelectrically.

    (13) See Tab A for proposed target locations.

4. <u>ADMINISTRATION AND LOGISTICS</u>

    a. See Annex P (Combat Service Support) to Operation Plan_____.

    b. Daily use of civilian labor emphasized. Details on transportation, messing, etc. in Annex P (Combat Service Support) to Operation Plan_____.

    c. Civilians may handle explosives in nonhazardous situations, but will NOT arm mines or charge explosives.

5. <u>COMMAND AND SIGNAL</u>

    a. See Annex K (Communications-Electronics).

    b. <u>Reports</u>

        (1) Minefields: report intent, initiation, and completion by fastest secure means; follow with standard required reports.

        (2) Demolitions and other obstacles: report location, type, completion time, and execution.

ACKNOWLEDGE RECEIPT

                    BY COMMAND OF _____

                                 Signature
                             Grade   Service
                                 Billet

TAB:

    A - MEF Barrier Location Concept (overlay)

<u>DISTRIBUTION</u>: See Annex Z (Distribution)

(Page number)

CLASSIFICATION

Engineer OPORD/OPLAN

CLASSIFICATION
(No change from oral orders)

Copy ___ of ___ copies
Issuing headquarters
PLACE OF ISSUE
Date/time of issue

OPORD (or OPLAN) _____

Ref: (a) Maps; Sheets, Series, Scale
     (b) Engineer Operations SOP

Time Zone: X

Task Organization. This is the engineer unit task organization. At the battalion level and lower, it is often clear enough in paragraph 3 that it does not need to be listed here.

1. SITUATION

   a. Enemy Forces. The S2 provides this based upon input from the maneuver G2/S2, other engineer staffs, and his own analysis. He covers aspects of terrain, weather, and threat maneuver, fire support, and engineer capability that significantly impact engineer operations. If discussion is lengthy, it goes into an intelligence annex and an overlay showing enemy positions, fortifications, obstacles, and terrain features (fords, tunnels, bridges, etc.). Cover any threat to engineer units operating in rear areas.

   b. Friendly Forces

      (1) State the mission of the supported maneuver force and the intent of the maneuver commander two levels up.

      (2) Describe engineer units that are in general support of the maneuver force. This is a brief statement of MAGTF engineer units that could be employed in the engineer unit's area of operations. For example, if a CSSE bridge company is in direct support of the GCE, the GCE's combat engineer commander needs to know that capability is available. The order could state: "Bridge Company, 8th Engineer Support Battalion, direct support to 2d MARDIV."

      (3) [As necessary] Describe other elements that can assist engineers, such as host nation territorial forces or forces that can deliver scatterable mines (artillery, Marine aviation, Air Force or Army aircraft).

(Page number)

CLASSIFICATION

Engineer OPORD/OPLAN

c. Attachments and Detachments

(1) Attachments. Cover any attachments to the engineer units. These can be engineer or other type units, such as an infantry platoon to assist in a flank mining mission. Include the DTG that attachment is effective.

(2) Detachments. These are subunits attached/OPCON to other units outside of the engineer unit and include those cross-attached to other engineer units in the area, like a division engineer platoon OPCON to the FSSG. Include the DTG that detachment is effective.

d. Assumptions. (OPLAN only).

2. MISSION

This is the restated engineer unit mission from the commander's estimate.

3. EXECUTION

a. Commander's Intent and Concept of Operations.

(1) Commander's Intent (Optional).

(2) Concept of Operations. This is a verbal description of the commander's scheme for accomplishing the unit's mission, using the elements under his control. (This does not include engineers attached or OPCON to maneuver forces.) It covers the entire operation from start to finish. It is specific to the particular operation and avoids overly broad generalities such as "priority to mobility, countermobility, then survivability in order." Refer as necessary to the operations overlay included with the order.

b. As necessary, use a subparagraph for each subordinate element remaining under unit control. List the tasks assigned to each. Give effective DTGs of task organization changes effecting any element under its subparagraph.

c. Coordinating Instructions. These apply to two or more subordinate elements. Cover mine uses or restrictions, if they are not already clear from the concept in paragraph 3a. When appropriate, describe the turnover of tasks between engineer units for breaches, obstacles, ford maintenance, etc. Do not include procedures already covered by doctrine or unit SOP. Coordinating instructions is the last paragraph in paragraph 3.

4. ADMINISTRATION AND LOGISTICS

If lengthy, put this information into an annex. Otherwise, the following format is useful but not required:

a. Material and Services. Give status on the classes of supply. Cover items that are command-controlled, particularly engineer related obstacle and construction materials (class IV). If applicable, give controlled supply rate (CSR) for engineer class V items. Also include any important information (including priorities) for transportation, services, and maintenance.

Engineer OPORD/OPLAN—Continued

CLASSIFICATION

    b. <u>Medical</u>. Specify the location of medical evacuation facilities in the unit's area.

    c. <u>Personnel</u>. Give priorities for replacement of casualties to support projected operations. Address EPW processing and location of collection points. Cover chaplain support if necessary.

    d. <u>Civil-Military</u>. Cover host nation support available, such as quarries, building supply centers, or equipment augmentation.

5. <u>COMMAND AND SIGNAL</u>

    a. <u>Command</u>. State the initial location of the unit commander and that of the unit CP (unless shown on the operations overlay). Give the projected displacement of the CP. Cover succession of command if different, from the unit SOP.

    b. <u>Signal</u>. As a minimum, list the communications-electronics operating instructions (CEOI) for the operation. State any signal restrictions, such as radio silence. Give the location of radio retransmission sites, if applicable. State any uses of smoke.

ACKNOWLEDGE RECEIPT

        BY COMMAND OF _____

                                Signature
                             Grade   Service
                                  Billet

ANNEXES: As needed (always include an operations overlay).

<u>DISTRIBUTION</u>: See Annex Z (Distribution).

(Page number)

CLASSIFICATION

Water Supply Plan

CLASSIFICATION

Copy no ____ of ____copies
Issuing Headquarters
PLACE OF ISSUE
Date/time of issue

APPENDIX _____ (Water) to ANNEX D (CSS) to Operation Order _____

Time Zone: X

1. GENERAL

    a. Purpose. Concise statement as to purpose of this appendix.

    b. Users. Statement as to what forces, organizations, or units this appendix is applicable (e.g., MEF, MEU, REGT, etc.).

2. WATER ANALYSIS

    a. Availability and condition of the raw water sources (e.g., fresh, brackish, saline, and how it will be treated) within the amphibious objective area. Estimate capability of existing water sources.

    b. Time-phased water consumption requirements for the organization preparing this appendix expressed in gallons per man per day (GMD) (e.g., D-day through D+5 - 5 GMD, D+6 through D+30 - 7 GMD) and the drinking water planning factors used.

    c. Estimated other bulk water requirements (e.g., bath, laundry, medical, vehicles).

    d. Estimate of total, time-phased water requirement (GMD) for the organization.

    e. Total water production capability of the organization.

    f. Total water storage and transportation capability of the organization. Identify storage/distribution systems or capability.

    g. Additional water sources (e.g., amphibious ships or other military forces).

3. WATER SUPPORT OPERATIONS

    a. Concept. Statement as to the concept of water support for the organization.

(Page number)

CLASSIFICATION

Water Supply Plan—Continued

CLASSIFICATION

      b. <u>Tasks</u>. Responsibilities of subordinate organizations with respect to water production, purification, distribution, and storage (e.g., ESBn, MWSS, medical battalion, and naval construction force tasks, and designation of landing force water manager).

        (1) Location of primary water production sites including host nation.

        (2) Water storage sites.

        (3) Landing force distribution scheme and responsibilities.

      e. <u>Other Facilities Requiring Water</u>. (e.g., hospitals, graves registration, etc.)

      f. <u>Coordinating Instructions</u>. Additional instructions relating to water support operations. Designation of landing force water manager.

4. <u>LIMITING FACTORS</u>

Describe limitations that could adversely affect water production, storage, distribution, or usage.

5. <u>ESTIMATE OF TIME-PHASED POTABLE WATER REQUIREMENTS AND PRODUCTION</u>

This part of the appendix may be prepared as TAB A or a brief summary of the total number of gallons required per day versus production, storage, and distribution capability. This can be used to provide data or allocation of resources. The following format may be used.

<u>Date</u> <u>Population Ashore</u> <u>Total Requirements</u> <u>Production</u> <u>Storage</u> <u>Distribution</u>

ACKNOWLEDGE RECEIPT

              BY COMMAND OF _____

                        Signature
                    Grade Service
                       Billet

TAB:

A - Potable Water Requirements (included)

<u>DISTRIBUTION</u>: See Annex Z (Distribution)

(Page number)

CLASSIFICATION

Water Supply Plan—Continued

CLASSIFICATION

TAB A (Potable Water Requirements) to APPENDIX _____(Water) to ANNEX D
(CSS) to Operation Order.

DAY	X	POPULATION ASHORE	X	DAILY GALLONS-PER-MAN REQUIREMENTS	=	DAILY WATER REQUIREMENTS ASHORE
D-DAY						
D + 1						
D + 2						
D + 3						
D + 4						
D + 5						
D + 6						
D + 7						
D + 8						
D + 9						
D + 10						
D + 11						
D + 12						
D + 13						
D + 14						
D + 15						

Both sustaining and minimum daily gallons-per-man requirements for various temperate zones are located in MCRP 4-25.5, *Bulk Liquids Operations* and FM 10-52, *Water Supply in Theaters of Operations.*

ACKNOWLEDGE RECEIPT

BY COMMAND OF _____

Signature
Grade   Service
Billet

(Page number)

CLASSIFICATION

Engineer Asset Summary

ENGINEER ASSET SUMMARY

UNIT	CO/PLT	MICLIC	M9ACE	D7DZR	SEE	CEV	VOLCANO	AVLB	MGB	RIBBON

Execution Matrix

ENGINEERS IN SUPPORT OF OFFENSIVE OPERATIONS
PE#2

EXECUTION MATRIX

MISSION:					
INTENT:					
ENG UNIT: CS/FREQ					
SPTD UNIT CS/FREQ					

TASK ORG
  SUB
  UNITS
 	
  SPECIAL
  EQUIP					

Mobility Capability Worksheet

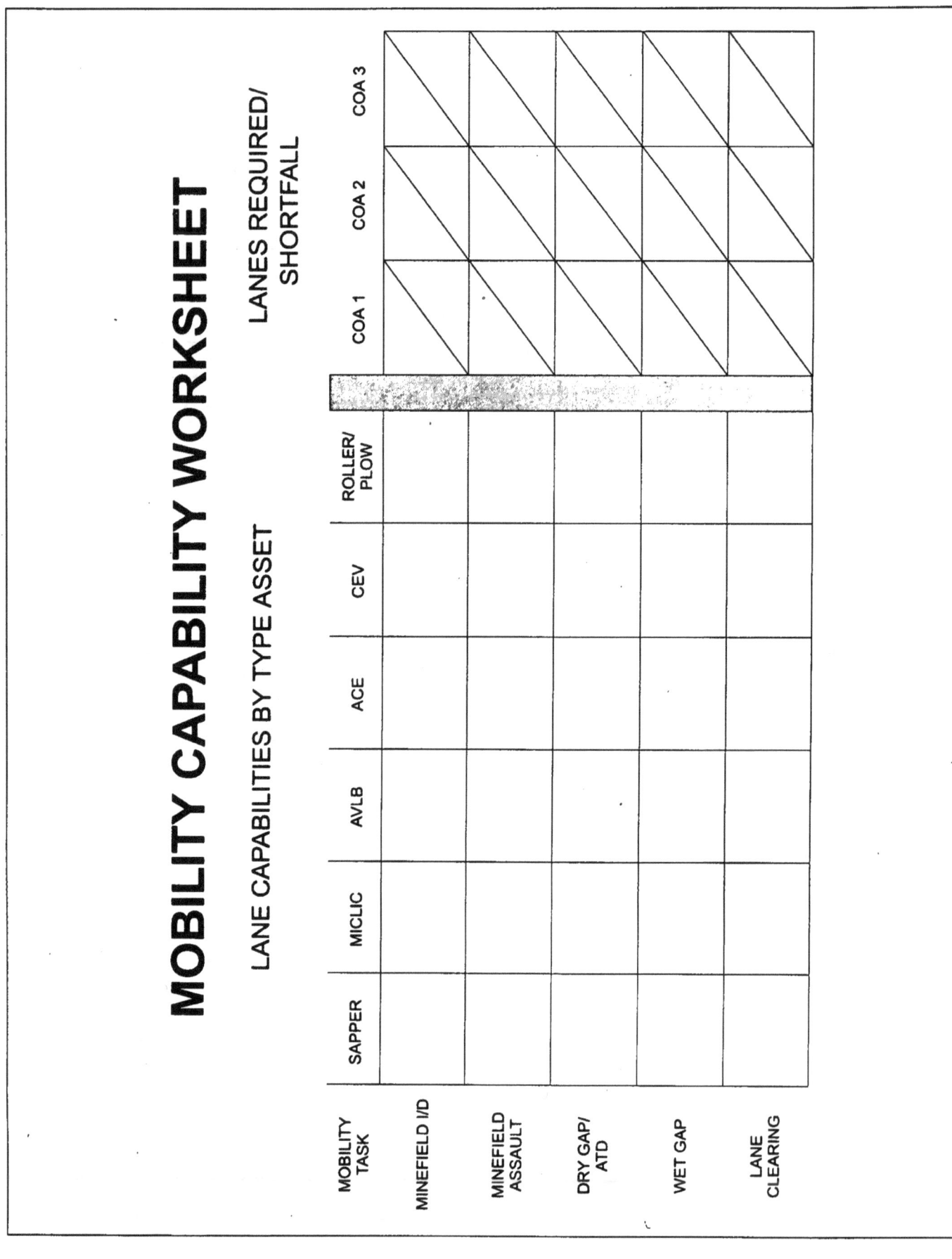

Countermobility Worksheet

ENGINEER ESTIMATE: DEFENSE
EBA/IPB: FRIENDLY M/CM/S CAPABILITY

COUNTERMOBILITY WORKSHEET

		TIME	ON HAND	OH/ & ALLOC	EFSP	COA 1	COA 2	COA 3	SHORTFALLS
DISRUPT	CONV								
	SCAT								
TURN	CONV								
	SCAT								
FIX	CONV								
	SCAT								
BLOCK	CONV								
	SCAT								

Blade Equivalent Triangle

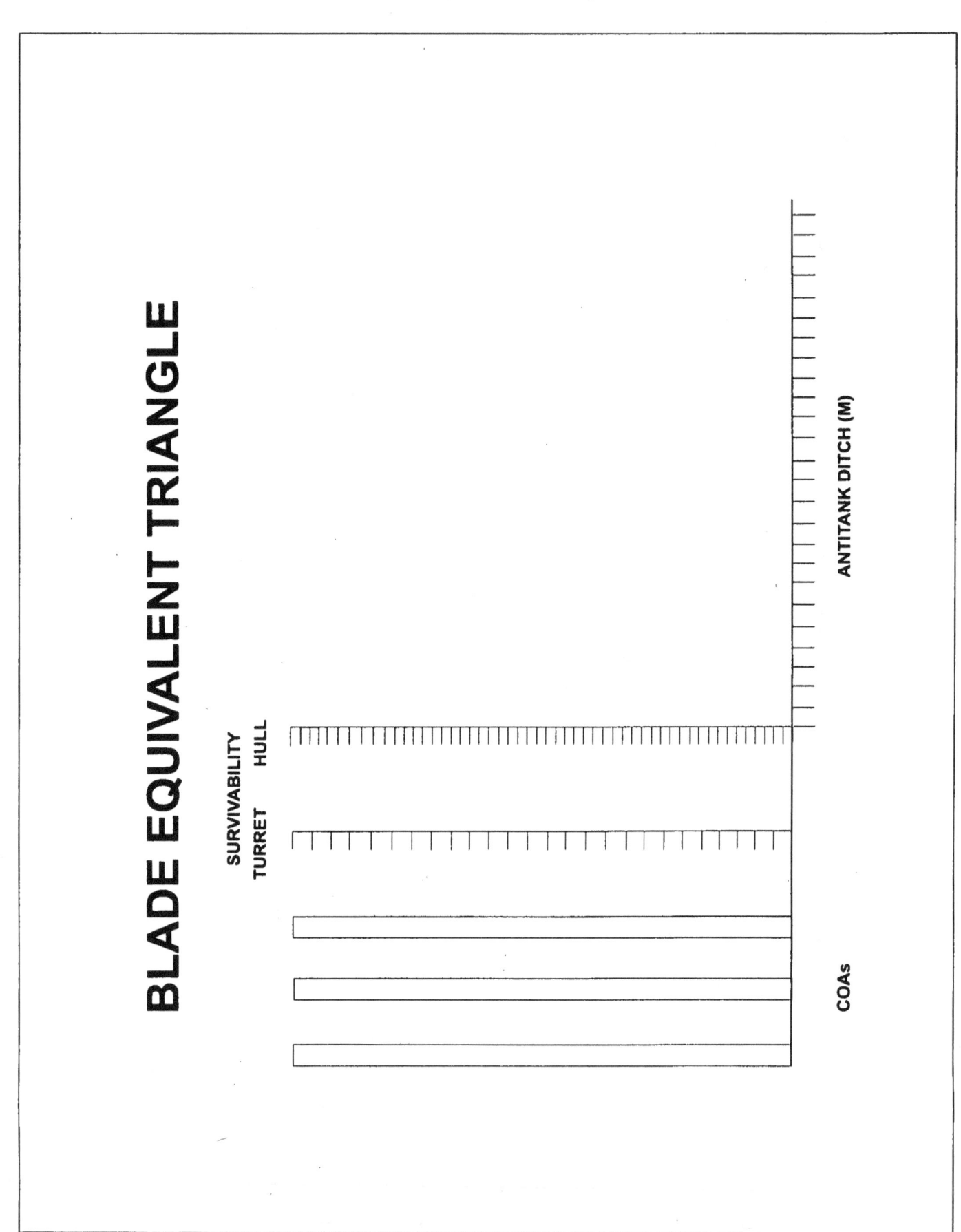

Survivability Quick Reference Chart

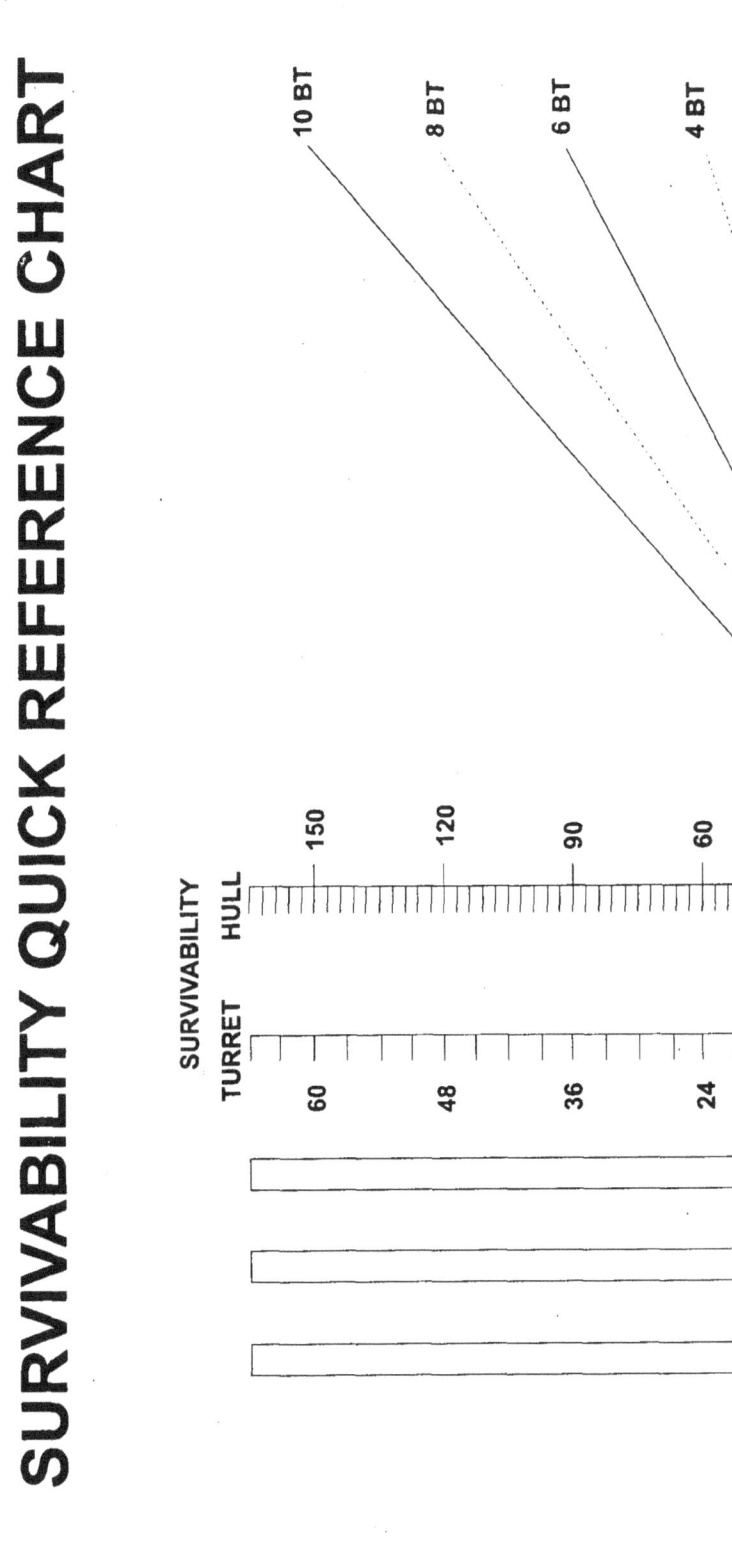

APPENDIX A

NATO STANAG 2036

<u>NATO STANAG 2036</u>
<u>LAND MINEFIELD LAYING, MARKING, RECORDING AND REPORTING</u>
<u>PROCEDURES</u>

The following information has been taken from NATO STANAG 2036 (Edition No. 4, Amendment 1). The aim of NATO STANAG 2036 is to standardize the policies, procedures, and techniques of land minefield laying, marking, recording and reporting for use by NATO forces, excluding policies, procedures, and techniques concerning employment of scatterable mines with a limited laid life, which are covered in ATP-50. Land minefield procedures cover the use of minefields on land, inland waterways and along beaches out to the extreme low-water line. However, this agreement does not include the laying, clearing, and marking of mines in harbors and inland waterways which have been internationally recognized as sea-going shipping routes.

6. <u>Minefield Policy</u>. The higher commands (corps and above) will decide the general guidelines on which land mine warfare is to be conducted. Orders from such commands should include permission to use mines, with restrictions, if any, areas which should or should not be mined, and the establishing at the same time of such priorities as necessary.

7. <u>Authority to Order the Laying of Minefields</u>. Commanders at division or brigade level may authorize or delegate the employment of minefields within the above guidelines with the exception of Drifting Mines, over which the higher command headquarters (corps and above) must exercise special control.

8. <u>Orders for Laying</u>. Orders issued by the commander authorized to order the laying of a minefield should contain at least the following details:

a. Tactical objective.

b. Type of minefield (antitank (AT), anti-personnel (AP), or mixed) and mode of emplacement.

c. Area to be mined, including gaps and minefield lanes if required.

d. Time by which the minefield must be effective.

e. Length of time for which the minefield must remain effective (if applicable).

f. Details as to the use of antilift devices.

g. Details of the type of marking and fencing required and the circumstances under which the marking and fencing should be removed.

h. The required mine density or minefield stopping power.

i. Reporting requirements.

NATO.........................
(Security Classification)

NATO STANAG 2036—Continued

9. Report of Intent/Completion. Commanders authorized to order minelaying will report their intention to lay a minefield to their next higher headquarters by the fastest secure means available. Report of completion will be forwarded by the fastest means possible upon completion of the minefield. These reports (which are not required from a division or higher level) will include the following information:

   a. Tactical objective.

   b. Type of minefield (AT, AP, or mixed) and mode of emplacement.

   c. Location of minefield, including location and width of minefield lanes and gaps.

   d. Length of time for which minefield will remain effective (if applicable).

   e. Estimated starting and completion times (for Report of Intent only).

   f. Actual completion time (for Report of Completion only).

10. Classification of Minefields and Laying Methods. Minefields are classified as Tactical, Nuisance, Protective, and Phoney minefields. These minefields may be employed against personnel, tracked and wheeled vehicles, air cushion craft, amphibious vehicles, and aircraft taxi-ing or hovering. The characteristics of all minefields are that they must be coordinated with the general fire plan and that they must be sited where they can be defended, guarded, or at least covered by observed friendly fire. The only exceptions to this general rule are nuisance minefields (paragraph 12 below).

11. Tactical Minefields.

   a. Tactical minefields, laid to a pattern with mines, buried or surface-laid, either by hand or by mechanical means, should conform with the patterns specified in Annex A. [of STANAG 2036 (the same information can be found in Field Manual (FM) 20-32 *Mine/Countermine Operations at the Company Level*).]

   b. Tactical minefields can also be laid without pattern.

12. Nuisance Minefields. Generally, nuisance minefields apply to restricted areas containing mines laid at random on enemy terrain or on terrain which may be abandoned to the enemy. They need not necessarily be covered by observation or fire.

13. Protective Minefields.

   a. Protective minefields are usually laid by order of the unit commander (independent platoon leader or higher).

   b. In order that the defensive position may be properly coordinated the unit commander laying the mines will normally send an "intention to lay" report (see paragraph 9).

NATO STANAG 2036—Continued

c. Mines will normally be laid on the surface, but may be buried if time and national policy permit.

d. The minefield will be marked or guarded in such a way that it will not endanger friendly troops.

e. Mines with antilift devices will not be used.

f. The minefield is covered by observation and direct fire by the protected unit.

g. It must be possible to provide routes around the minefield or lanes through it, in order to avoid delaying the passage of friendly forces.

h. On leaving the position, the unit commander will report whether the mines have been lifted or left in place. If the minefield is left in place, the battalion or equivalent sized unit will submit to the higher unit staff a minefield report to enable the engineer operations staff to keep the overall obstacles plan up to date. The engineer operations staff will attach this report to a minefield record form and distribute the record as specified in paragraph 19.c. of this STANAG. The minefield report must at least include:

(1) Location of the minefield (UTM-coordinates).

(2) Number and types of mines; mode of emplacement.

(3) Size of the minefield.

14. Phoney Minefields. The effectiveness of a phoney minefield depends upon its resemblance to the type of minefield being simulated. The phoney minefield must not contain any live mines and will be marked. Phoney minefields are measured as in paragraph 18.e. and recorded in paragraph 19.

15. Marking and Fencing of Minefields.

a. In principle all areas in friendly territory containing mines will be marked by signs and, if possible, be fenced in accordance with Annexes D and E (with the exception of protective minefields). Whether or not fencing and signs should be removed before abandoning minefields to the enemy should be decided by the authorized commander.

b. The method of marking and fencing in forward areas of operations will be at the discretion of the authorizing commander.

c. Minefields emplaced in or along inland waterways and banks are to be marked on the bank in the same manner as on land (per Appendix 6 to Annex E).

d. Marking of minefields emplaced on beaches must be coordinated with the naval commander responsible for the sea area.

e. Remotely delivered minefields in enemy terrain are not normally marked.

NATO STANAG 2036—Continued

f. Marking/fencing should be removed from all minefields that are certain to be inert unless they are retained as phoney minefields.

16. Marking and Fencing of Minefield Lanes. All minefield lanes will normally be fenced on both sides with the fences linking with the minefield perimeter marking (or fencing) at entrances and exits. In addition, lane entrances and exits, as well as the lane itself, should be marked with signs to indicate the safe and dangerous sides respectively. Lane markers should be visible at all times including periods of poor visibility (see Annex E). The type of marking, fencing, and illumination of minefield lanes in the forward area of operations will be at the discretion of the authorized commander. Lanes in areas mined with scatterable mines will exist only as ground that has not been mined between or adjacent to the limits of marked minefields.

17. Recording of Minefields. The following general principles apply:

   a. Distances on the minefield record form will be recorded in metres. Pace measurements using the normal pace of approximately 3/4 of a metre may be used to acquire that dimension. The system of measurement used must be mentioned in the notes of the minefield record.

   b. Direction will be indicated in degrees of angular measurement (1/360) clockwise from magnetic North. When using a different measuring unit, it must be so stated in the minefield record.

   c. Suitable aerial photographs showing markings and terrain features which are also identifiable on the map may be used instead of the minefield diagram or supplements to the minefield diagram.

   d. If a minefield diagram (or air photograph) is created as a separate document to the heading sheet of the minefield record, all documents are to be firmly affixed together. A description of the total record is to be made under notes on the front side of the Minefield Record Form.

18. Measurement of Minefields.

   a. Random laid minefields are identified in terms of the minefield corner points, density, buffer distance, type of mine and self-destruct time, if applicable.

   b. Pattern minefields with buried mines laid by hand will normally be "measured-in-whole", as shown at Appendix 2 to Annex B.

   c. Pattern minefields with surface-laid or mechanically buried mines may be "measured-in-whole" or "measured-in-part", as shown at Appendix 3 and Appendix 4 to Annex B.

   d. When employing horizontal action mines, which have a limited area of effect, the direction of action will be indicated by an arrow symbol.

NATO STANAG 2036—Continued

NATO...........................
(Security Classification)

e. Phoney minefields are measured in terms of the coordinates of the minefield's boundaries.

19. <u>Minefield Record</u>.

    a. Minefield records must be prepared by the laying unit for each minefield (except protective minefields, see paragraph 13.h.) utilizing an appropriate form. The record provides the location and design of the minefield to assist friendly troops in locating and clearing it, and in the case of self-neutralizing mines, will indicate the effective life of the minefield to assist in the planning of tactical movements. Remotely delivered minefields will be recorded in terms of minefield corner points, density, self-destruct times and buffer distance.

    b. Several nuisance minefields near to each other may be entered on one minefield record, if size permits, as shown at Appendix 7 to Annex B.

    c. The minefield record will be forwarded by the laying unit. One copy of the minefield record will be retained at the next higher command, one copy at corps, where appropriate, and one copy at the proper national territorial authority.

    d. After completion, the minimum security classification of the minefield record is NATO RESTRICTED or the national equivalent.

    e. If mines are delivered into an already existing minefield which has been laid to a standard pattern, the original minefield record will be retained; however, the additional information on the mines laid at random will be entered on the minefield record.

20. <u>Minefield Record Submission</u>. Immediately upon completion of the minefield, the minefield record (Annex B) will be submitted in accordance with paragraph 19.c. above.

21. <u>Safety Distances</u>. Although mine strips/rows may be laid using paces, all safety distances must be established in metres (see Annex A of STANAG 2036 or FM 20-32 for more information).

22. <u>Enemy or Unidentified Minefields</u>. Any unmarked or unrecorded minefield will be treated as an enemy minefield. Reporting these minefields is accomplished according to the national or command procedures. Further action, such as recording, marking or clearing will be the responsibility of the authorized commander.

NATO...........................
(Security Classification)

NATO STANAG 2036, Annex B

ANNEX B TO
STANAG 2036
(Edition 4)

MINEFIELD RECORD FORMS

Appendices to this Annex illustrate completed minefield records depicting the method of recording various minefields. These appendices are:

Appendices: 1. Minefield Record Form.

2. Minefield Record Form (completed for Standard Pattern Minefield, Buried, Laid by Hand).

3. Minefield Record Form (completed for Pattern (Row) Minefield, Surface-Laid). This example can be applied to buried, laid by hand also.

4. Minefield Record Form (completed for Minefield, Buried, Mechanically Laid).

5. Minefield Record Form (completed for Minefield, Random, Surface-Laid).

6. Minefield Record Form (completed for Minefield in Waterway and on Banks, Random, Surface-Laid).

7. Minefield Record Form (completed for Nuisance Minefield, Buried).

NATO STANAG 2036, Appendix 1 To Annex B

MINEFIELD RECORD FORM (Front)

NATO UNCLASSIFIED

APPENDIX 1 TO ANNEX B TO STANAG 2036
(Edition 4)

MINEFIELD RECORD

NATO.........................   COPY .... OF ....
(Security classification when filled)   SHEET NO. .... OF ....

AUTHORITY: MINEFIELD NUMBER:
LAYING UNIT: MAP:SERIES, NO AND SCALE:
OFFICER IN CHARGE: SHEET NO.(OR NAME):

START:
COMPLETION:
RECORDER:

DATE AND TIME

LANDMARKS

NO.	COORDINATES	DESCRIPTION
1		
2		
3		
4		

INTERMEDIATE MARKERS

NO.	DESCRIPTION
1	
2	
3	
4	

DESCRIPTION OF BOUNDARY FENCE OR MARKING

LANES

NO.	WIDTH	HOW MARKED	METHOD OF CLOSING
1			
2			
3			

NO. OF STRIPS/ROWS.......DESCRIPTION OF STRIP/ROW MARKERS:

NOTES

1. MINE CLUSTERS AT.............................METRES/SPACES SPACING
....
....
....

TACTICAL MINEFIELD NUISANCE MINEFIELD PHONEY MINEFIELD		ANTITANK MINES (AT)						ANTIPERSONNEL MINES					
		TYPE	TYPE	TYPE	TYPE	TYPE	TOTAL AT MINES	ANTI-LIFT DEV	TYPE	TYPE	TYPE	TOTAL AP MINES	
		NO.	NO.	NO.	NO.	NO.	NO.	NO.	NO.	NO.	NO.	NO.	
BURIED AND	IOE A												
	B												
SURFACE LAID	C												
	D												
IN STRIPS	E												
IN ROWS	F												
	G												
W/O PATTERN	H												
	J												
TOTAL													

M I N E S

SIGNATURE (OFFICER IN CHARGE)...................
DATE:............................

NATO..........................

NATO UNCLASSIFIED

NATO STANAG 2036, Appendix 1 To Annex B—Continued

NATO UNCLASSIFIED

LOCATION OF ENEMY | MAGNETIC NORTH

LEGEND

example: 150/20 indicates azimuth/distance
scale: 1 cm = _____ m METRES.
UNLESS OTHERWISE STATED ALL ANGLES ARE MAGNETIC BEARINGS USING 360°
COMPASS. INDICATE ALTERNATIVE IF USED:

64 PTS	6400 MILS	400 GRADS	OTHER

ALL DISTANCES ARE MEASURED IN METRES.
INDICATE SYSTEM OF MEASUREMENT USED:

PACING (0.75M)	CLOTH 100M TAPE	STEEL 100M TAPE	OTHER

SIGNATURE.................

NATO.............
Security classification when filled

MINEFIELD RECORD FORM (BACK)

NATO.............
Security classification when filled

NATO UNCLASSIFIED

NATO STANAG 2036, Appendix 2 To Annex B

NATO UNCLASSIFIED

APPENDIX 2 TO ANNEX B TO STANAG 2036
(Edition 4)

COPY ......1...... OF ....5......
SHEET NO .....1...... OF ....1......

EXAMPLE: Standard Pattern Minefield, Buried, Laid by Hand
MINEFIELD RECORD FORM (Front)

MINEFIELD RECORD

NATO ....CONFIDENTIAL....
(Security classification when filled)

DATE AND TIME	START: 231300Z Jun 82
	COMPLETION: 241000Z Jun 82

RECORDER: SSG Winchester

MINEFIELD NUMBER: 28XX(Inf)-1-E
MAP: SERIES, NO AND SCALE: M754, 1:50,000
SHEET NO.(OR NAME): L7542 PFARRKIRCHEN

AUTHORITY: CG, 28 Inf Div (Mech)
LAYING UNIT: 3 Engr Regt
OFFICER IN CHARGE: CPT Mooneyhan

LANDMARKS

NO.	COORDINATES	DESCRIPTION
1	ZZ 3001768l	East corner of Bridge Abutment at Kollbach
2	ZZ 30097671	West corner of Building
3		
4		

INTERMEDIATE MARKERS

NO.	DESCRIPTION
1	Three short "U" pickets, extending 12 inches
XXXX	above ground, wrapped with 3 strands of barbed
XXXX	wire.
2	Tree with 3 wraps of barbed wire at base.

DESCRIPTION OF BOUNDARY FENCE OR MARKING
STANDARD, COMPLETELY SURROUNDING MINEFIELD

LANES

NO.	WIDTH	HOW MARKED	METHOD OF CLOSING
1	5 Metres	Wire fence & signs	5 AT mines, 5 AP
XXX			mines stored at
XXX			ZZ 30117671

NO. OF STRIPS/ROWS....3....DESCRIPTION OF STRIP/ROW MARKERS:
2"X2" wooden stakes driven flush with ground with an 8 penny nail driven in the top

		ANTITANK MINES (AT)										ANTIPERSONNEL MINES					TOTAL AP MINES
		TYPE DM 11	TYPE	TYPE	TYPE	TYPE	TYPE	TYPE	TOTAL AT MINES	APT. LIFT DEV	TYPE DM-11	TYPE DM-31	TYPE	TYPE		
TACTICAL MINEFIELD NUISANCE MINEFIELD PHONEY MINEFIELD		NO.	NO.	NO.	NO.	NO.	NO.	NO.		NO.	NO.	NO.	NO.	NO.		NO.
BURIED AND	IOE	28							28	0	84	0				84
	A	93							93	4	186	93				279
SURFACE LAID	B	95							95	5	190	190				380
	C	96							96	5	192	192				384
	D															
IN STRIPS	E															
	F															
IN ROWS	G															
	H															
W/O PATTERN	J															
TOTAL		312							312	14	652	475				1,127

NOTES

1. MINE CLUSTERS AT ....6..................
2. IOE. Live. Clusters. (all others are numbered but
   omitted)..I1:...1, 2, 3, 5, 6............... I2....2, 3, 4, 5, 6.
   I3....1, 2, 4, 6, 7, 8, 9, 10.......... I4....1, 3, 5, 6, 8.
   I5....1, 2, 3, 5, 6.
3. ....Numbered. Omitted. Clusters...in. Regular. Strips.....a-53, 87.
   .B-None...C-73.
4. Clusters. w/anti-lift. devices. (ALL-M-5. type).....IOE.........
   .None...A-7, 38, 85, 93............. B-9, 44, 63, 71............. C-2, 18, 58
5. Clusters. w/tripwire. activated. AP. Mines:.....NONE.
6. Strip. Cluster...Composition...IOE - 1:3:0............. B - 1:2:2.
   ......A - 1:2:1. .... C - 1:2:2.
7. All. safety. pins/clips. buried. 30cm. to. rear. of. start. row. marker.

................METRES/PACES. SPACING...................

SIGNATURE (OFFICER IN CHARGE).........................
DATE:.......................

NATO .... CONFIDENTIAL ....

NATO UNCLASSIFIED

NATO STANAG 2036, Appendix 2 to Annex B—Continued

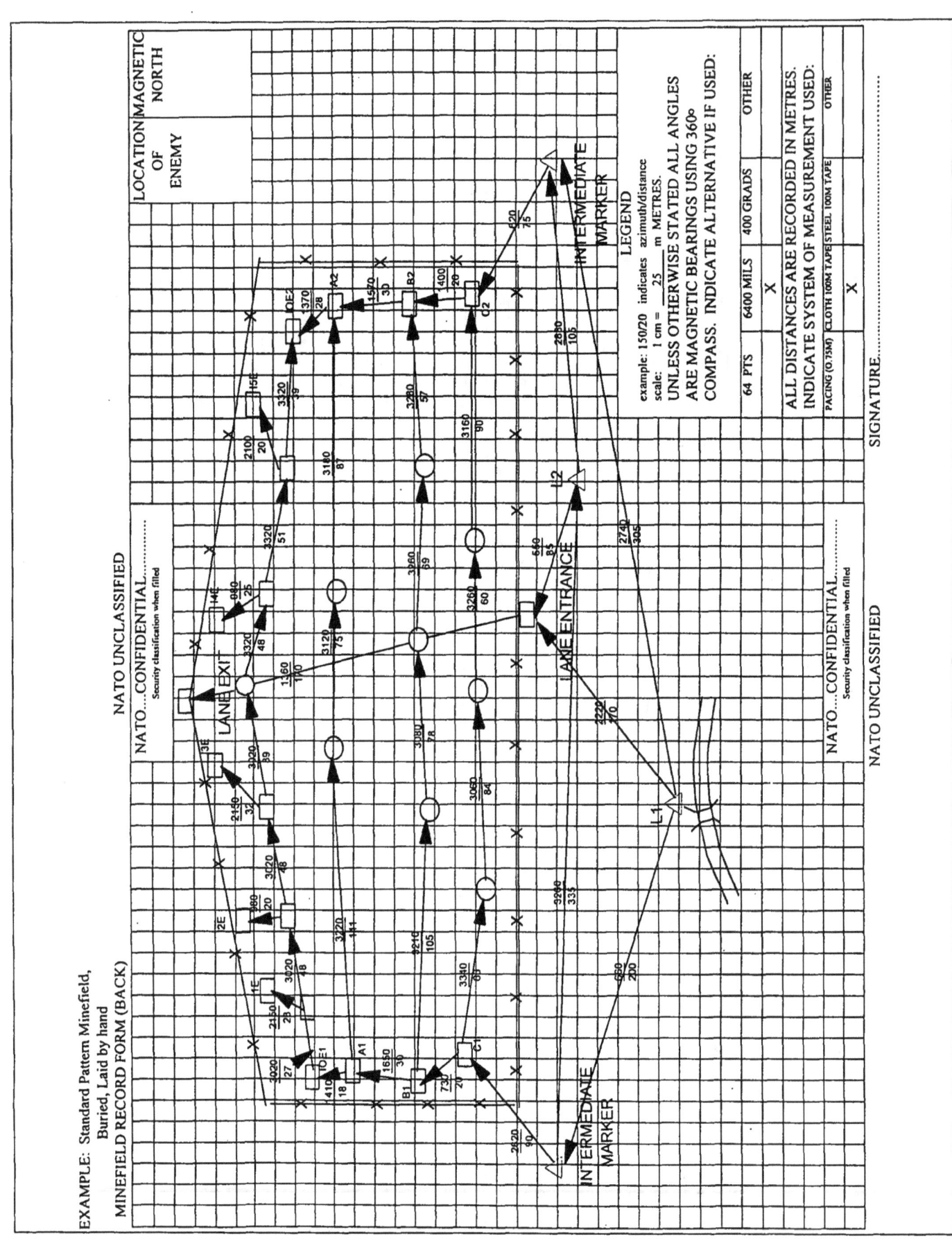

NATO STANAG 2036, Appendix 3 to Annex B

EXAMPLE: Pattern (Row) Minefield, Surface Laid

MINEFIELD RECORD FORM (Front)

NATO UNCLASSIFIED

APPENDIX 3 TO ANNEX B TO STANAG 2036
(Edition 4)

MINEFIELD RECORD

NATO ... CONFIDENTIAL .....
(Security classification when filled)

COPY ...... 1 .... OF .... 5 ....
SHEET NO. .... 1 .... OF .... 1 ....

MINEFIELD NUMBER: 28XX(Inf)-3-E
MAP: SERIES, NO AND SCALE: M745, 1:50,000
SHEET NO. (OR NAME): L7542

		DATE AND TIME
	START: 241310Z Jun 82	
	COMPLETION: 241800Z Jun 82	

AUTHORITY: CG, 28 Inf Div (Mech)
LAYING UNIT: 3 Engr Regt
OFFICER IN CHARGE: CPT Mooneyhan
RECORDER: SSG Winchester

LANDMARKS

NO.	COORDINATES	DESCRIPTION
1	ZZ 49997305	North-East corner of Warehouse
2	ZZ 50257315	"U" picket driven flush w/ground, center of road junction
XXXX		
XXXX		

INTERMEDIATE MARKERS

NO.	DESCRIPTION
1	
2	
3	
4	

DESCRIPTION OF BOUNDARY FENCE OR MARKING
STANDARD, COMPLETELY SURROUNDING MINEFIELD

LANES

NO.	WIDTH	HOW MARKED	METHOD OF CLOSING
1			
2			
3			

NO. OF STRIPS/ROWS...3...DESCRIPTION OF STRIP/ROW MARKERS:
"U" picket driven flush with the ground

TACTICAL MINEFIELD NUISANCE MINEFIELD PHONEY MINEFIELD		ANTITANK MINES (AT)											ANTIPERSONNEL MINES			
		TYPE DM II	TYPE	TYPE	TYPE	TYPE	TOTAL AT MDRS	ANT-LIFT DEV	TYPE	TYPE	TYPE	TOTAL AP MDRS			
		NO.	NO.	NO.	NO.	NO.	NO.	NO.	NO.	NO.	NO.	NO.			
BURIED AND	IOE														
	A	48					48								
	B	44					44								
SURFACE LAID	C	50					50								
	D														
IN STRIPS	E														
	F														
IN ROWS	G														
	H														
W/O PATTERN	J														
TOTAL		142					142								

M I N E S

NOTES

1. MINE CLUSTERS AT.............6.............METRES/PACES SPACING
2. ..IOE. Live. Clusters:............. NONE.
3. ..Numbered. Omitted. Clusters..in. Regular. Strips...NONE.
4. ..Clusters..w/Anti-lift. Devices. NONE.
5. ..Clusters..w/tripwire..activated..AP..Mines:...NONE.
6. ..Strip..Cluster..Composition...Single DM 11 AT Mine.
7. All..Safety. Pins/Clips..are..buried. 30cm..to..Rear..of..Start. Row. Markers.
8. ..Mechanical. Surface. Laid. Hasty. Camouflage. Used.

SIGNATURE (OFFICER IN CHARGE)...............................
DATE: ...... 24..June..1982.............

NATO ..........CONFIDENTIAL.....

NATO UNCLASSIFIED

NATO STANAG 2036, Appendix 3 to Annex B—Continued

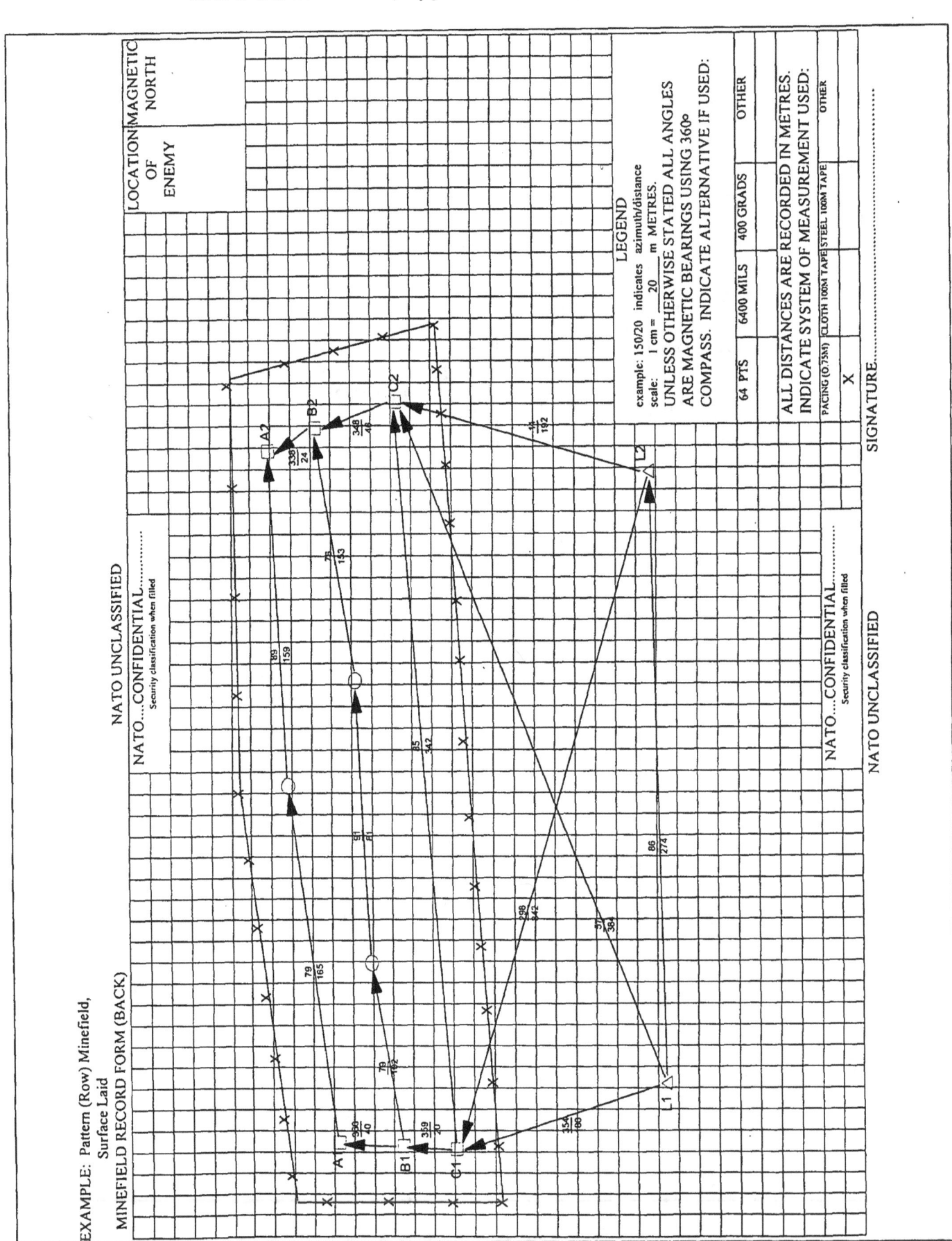

NATO STANAG 2036, Appendix 4 to Annex B

EXAMPLE: MINEFIELD, BURIED, MECHANICALLY LAID

NATO UNCLASSIFIED

APPENDIX 4 TO ANNEX B TO STANAG 2036
(Edition 4)

MINEFIELD RECORD FORM (Front)

MINEFIELD RECORD

NATO....CONFIDENTIAL....
(Security classification when filled)

COPY ....1.... OF ....5....
SHEET NO ....1.... OF ....1....

MINEFIELD NUMBER: 28XX(Inf)-2-E
MAP:SERIES, NO AND SCALE: M745, 1:50,000
SHEET NO.(OR NAME): KLEINECK

AUTHORITY: CG, 28 Inf Div (Mech)	DATE AND TIME	START: 231300Z Jun 82
LAYING UNIT: 3 Engr Regt		COMPLETION: 241000Z Jun 82
OFFICER IN CHARGE: CPT Mooneyhan		RECORDER: SSG Winchester

LANDMARKS

NO.	COORDINATES	DESCRIPTION
1	ZZ 30027681	East corner of Warehouse
2	ZZ 30047681	West corner of Bridge
3		
4		

INTERMEDIATE MARKERS

NO.	DESCRIPTION
1	
2	
3	
4	

DESCRIPTION OF BOUNDARY FENCE OR MARKING
STANDARD. COMPLETELY SURROUNDING MINEFIELD

NO. OF STRIPS/ROWS...3...DESCRIPTION OF STRIP/ROW MARKERS:

LANES

NO.	WIDTH	HOW MARKED	METHOD OF CLOSING
1	8 metres	Single cable	Mines at Grid
		staked to ground	ZZ 30327652
XXXX		marking the east side	
XXXX			

TACTICAL MINEFIELD / NUISANCE MINEFIELD / PHONEY MINEFIELD

		ANTITANK MINES (AT)								ANTIPERSONNEL MINES									
		TYPE	TYPE	NO.	TYPE	NO.	ANTI LIFT DEV	TOTAL AT MINES	TYPE	NO.	TYPE	NO.	TYPE	NO.	TYPE	NO.	TOTAL AP MINES
		DM 11															
		NO.		NO.		NO.			NO.		NO.		NO.		NO.		
BURIED AND	IOE																
M I N E S	A	40						40									
	B	39						39									
SURFACE LAID	C	42						42									
	D																
IN STRIPS	E																
	F																
IN ROWS	G																
	H																
W/O PATTERN	J																
TOTAL		121						121									

NOTES

1. MINE CLUSTERS AT....5.5....METRES/PACES SPACING
2. IOE Live Clusters:.....None.
3. Numbered Omitted Clusters in Regular Strips... None.
4. Clusters w/Anti-lift Devices NONE.
5. Clusters w/tripwire activated AP Mines.....None.
6. Strip Cluster Composition: L9A1 AT Mine Only.
7. All safety pins/clips are buried 30cm to rear of start row marker.
8. Mechanically laid buried at 5.5m spacing in each row.
9. Distances between mines clusters measured by mine counter Other distances measured by 100m cable.

SIGNATURE (OFFICER IN CHARGE)...........
DATE:....24 June 82...........

NATO.........CONFIDENTIAL...........

NATO UNCLASSIFIED

NATO STANAG 2036, Appendix 4 to Annex B—Continued

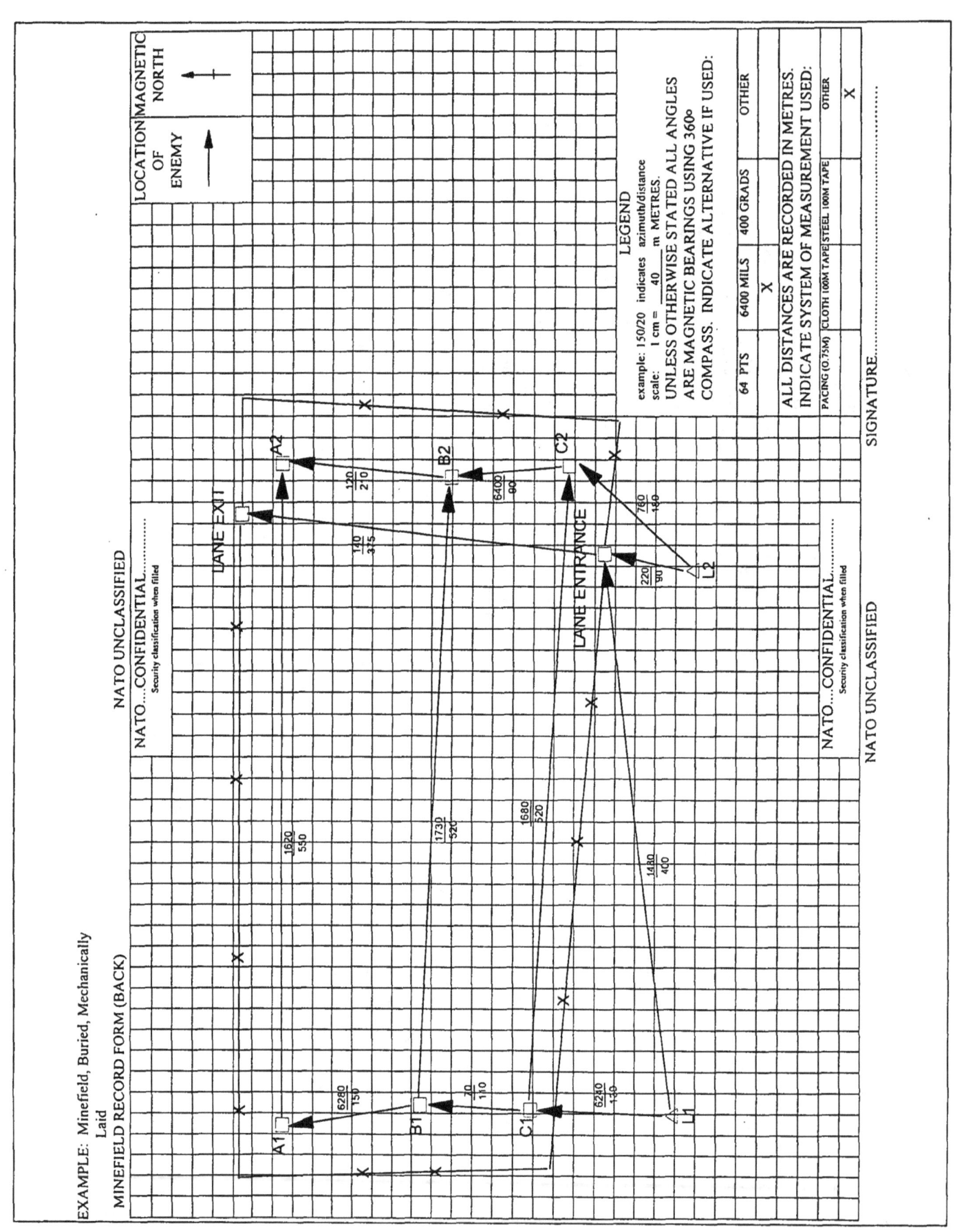

EXAMPLE: Minefield, Buried, Mechanically
Laid

MINEFIELD RECORD FORM (BACK)

NATO STANAG 2036, Appendix 5 to Annex B

EXAMPLE: Minefield, Random, Surface Laid

MINEFIELD RECORD FORM (Front)

NATO UNCLASSIFIED

APPENDIX 5 TO ANNEX B TO STANAG 2036
(Edition 4)

MINEFIELD RECORD

NATO...SECRET.....
(Security classification when filled)

COPY .....1..... OF ....5.......
SHEET NO .....1..... OF ....2.......

MINEFIELD NUMBER: T38
MAP: SERIES, NO AND SCALE: M745, 1:50,000
SHEET NO (OR NAME): L7542 (PFARRKIRCHEN)

AUTHORITY: CG, 28 Inf Div (Mech)
LAYING UNIT: 3 Engr Regt
OFFICER IN CHARGE: CPT Berger

DATE AND TIME	START: 251310Z Jun 82
	COMPLETION: 251700Z Jun 82
	RECORDER: SGT Runde

LANDMARKS

NO.	COORDINATES	DESCRIPTION
1	ZZ 45827365	North East corner, Bridge Abutment
2		
3		
4		

INTERMEDIATE MARKERS

NO.	DESCRIPTION
1	
2	
3	
4	

DESCRIPTION OF BOUNDARY FENCE OR MARKING

Corner points (P1, P2, P3, P4) are 2 inch wooden stakes protruding 5cm from surface level

NO. OF STRIPS/ROWS...... DESCRIPTION OF STRIP/ROW MARKERS:

LANES

NO.	WIDTH	HOW MARKED	METHOD OF CLOSING
1			
2			
3			

NOTES

1. MINE CLUSTERS AT...... METRES/PACES SPACING
2. DROPPED. FROM. HELICOPTER. 80. Knots. at. 100ft.
3. CORNER. POINTS. OF. MINEFIELD. PLACED. PRIOR. TO. DROP.
   P1. (ZZ. 45877381). P2. (ZZ. 46087378). P3. (ZZ. 46107383).
   P4. (ZZ. 45897386).
4. A. PHOTOGRAPH. IS. ATTACHED. OF. THE. AREA. (SHEET. 2).
5. SELF. DESTRUCT. SET. FOR271600Z. Jun.

TACTICAL MINEFIELD
NUISANCE MINEFIELD
PHONEY MINEFIELD

		ANTITANK MINES (AT)						ANTIPERSONNEL MINES					
		TYPE	TYPE	TYPE	TYPE	TYPE	TOTAL AT MINES	ANTI-LIFT DEV	TYPE	TYPE	TYPE	TOTAL AP MINES
		M 56										
		NO.	NO.	NO.	NO.	NO.		NO.	NO.	NO.	NO.	NO.
BURIED AND	IOE A	320					320					
	B											
SURFACE LAID	C											
	D											
IN STRIPS	E											
	F											
IN ROWS	G											
	H											
W/O PATTERN	J											
TOTAL		320					320					

M I N E S

SIGNATURE (OFFICER IN CHARGE).....................
DATE.......25...June79.......................

NATO..........SECRET......

NATO UNCLASSIFIED

NATO STANAG 2036, Appendix 5 to Annex B—Continued

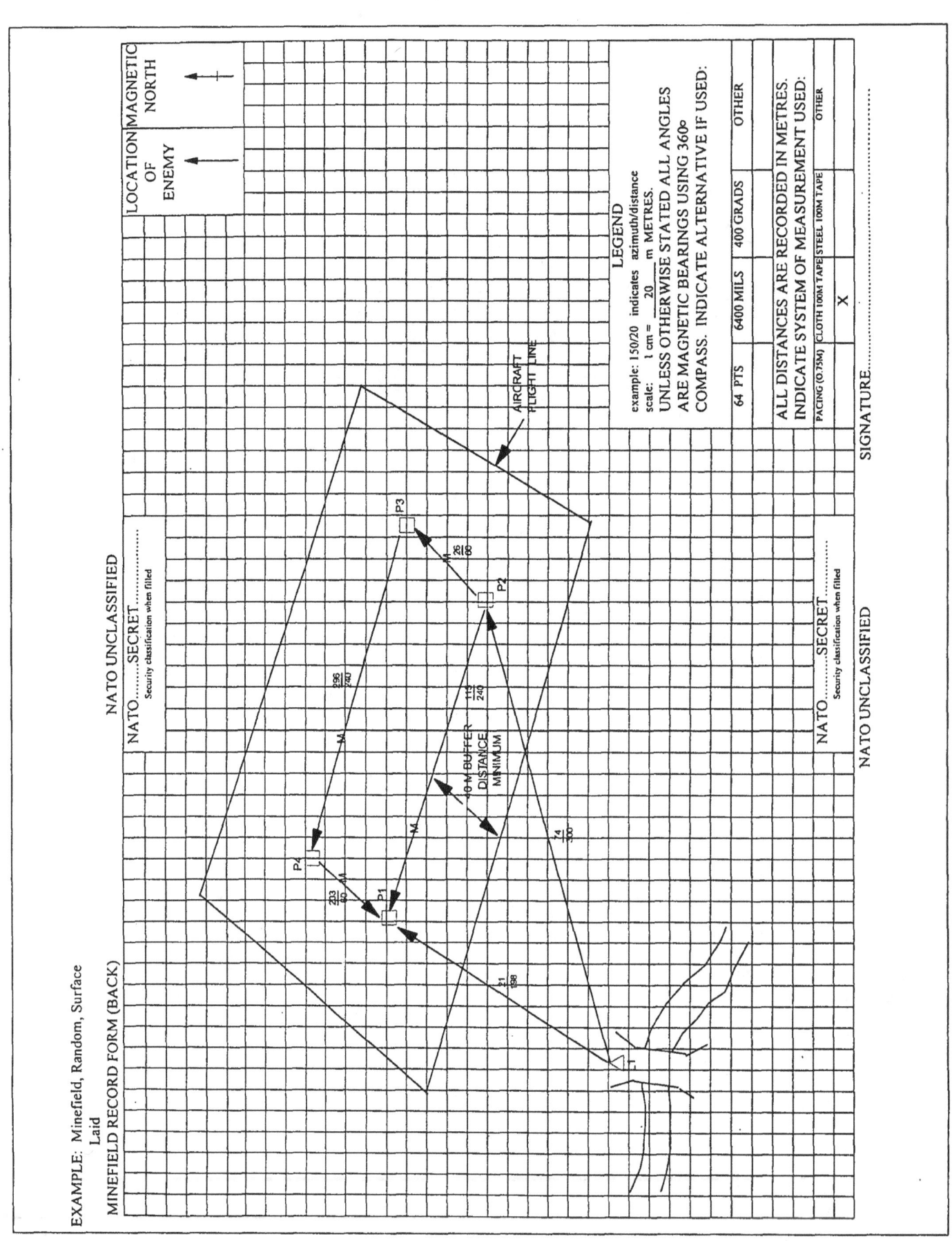

NATO STANAG 2036, Appendix 6 to Annex B

EXAMPLE: Minefield in Waterway and
on Banks, Random, Surface-Laid

MINEFIELD RECORD FORM (Front)

NATO UNCLASSIFIED

MINEFIELD RECORD

APPENDIX 6 TO ANNEX B TO STANAG 2036
(Edition 4)

COPY ....1...... OF ....5.....
SHEET NO ....1..... OF ....1.....

NATO....CONFIDENTIAL......
(Security classification when filled)

DATE AND TIME	START: 251310Z Jun 82
	COMPLETION: 251700Z Jun 82

MINEFIELD NUMBER: T51
MAP: SERIES, NO AND SCALE: M745, 1:50,000
SHEET NO.(OR NAME): L7542 (PFARRKIRCHEN)

AUTHORITY: CG, 28 Inf Div (Mech)
LAYING UNIT: 3 Engr Regt
OFFICER IN CHARGE: CPT Berger
RECORDER: SGT Runde

LANDMARKS

NO.	COORDINATES	DESCRIPTION
1	ZZ 45872736	West Corner Road Fork
2	ZZ 46137367	Expedient Landmark (Pickets)
3		
4		

INTERMEDIATE MARKERS

NO.	DESCRIPTION
1	
2	
3	
4	

DESCRIPTION OF BOUNDARY FENCE OR MARKING
WIRE FENCING AND SIGNS WITH LIGHTS

LANES

NO.	WIDTH	HOW MARKED	METHOD OF CLOSING
1			
2			
3			

NO. OF STRIPS/ROWS ...... DESCRIPTION OF STRIP/ROW MARKERS:

TACTICAL MINEFIELD			ANTITANK MINES (AT)								ANTIPERSONNEL MINES							
NUISANCE MINEFIELD			TYPE	TYPE	TYPE	TYPE	TYPE	TYPE	TOTAL AT MINES	ANTI LIFT DEV	TYPE	TYPE	TYPE	TYPE	TOTAL AP MINES		
PHONEY MINEFIELD			DM11														
			NO.	NO.	NO.	NO.	NO.	NO.	NO.	NO.	NO.	NO.	NO.	NO.	NO.		
	BURIED AND	A	270						270						270		
		B															
	SURFACE LAID	C															
		D															
M I N E S	IN STRIPS	E															
		F															
	IN ROWS	G															
		H															
	W/O PATTERN	J															
	IOE																
	TOTAL		270						270						270		

NOTES

1. MINE CLUSTERS AT .... METRES/PACES SPACING
2. Laid from boat in water, 120 mines.
3. Laid on bank, 150 mines.
4. River navigable by ships (not recognized as a seagoing shipping route).
5. Corner Points.
   P1 ZZ 45767383
   P2 ZZ 46207381
   P3 ZZ 46117400 (Navigation Marker)
   P4 ZZ 45797396 (Navigation Marker)

SIGNATURE (OFFICER IN CHARGE)...............
DATE: ......25 June79................

NATO......CONFIDENTIAL..........

NATO UNCLASSIFIED

NATO STANAG 2036, Appendix 6 to Annex B—Continued

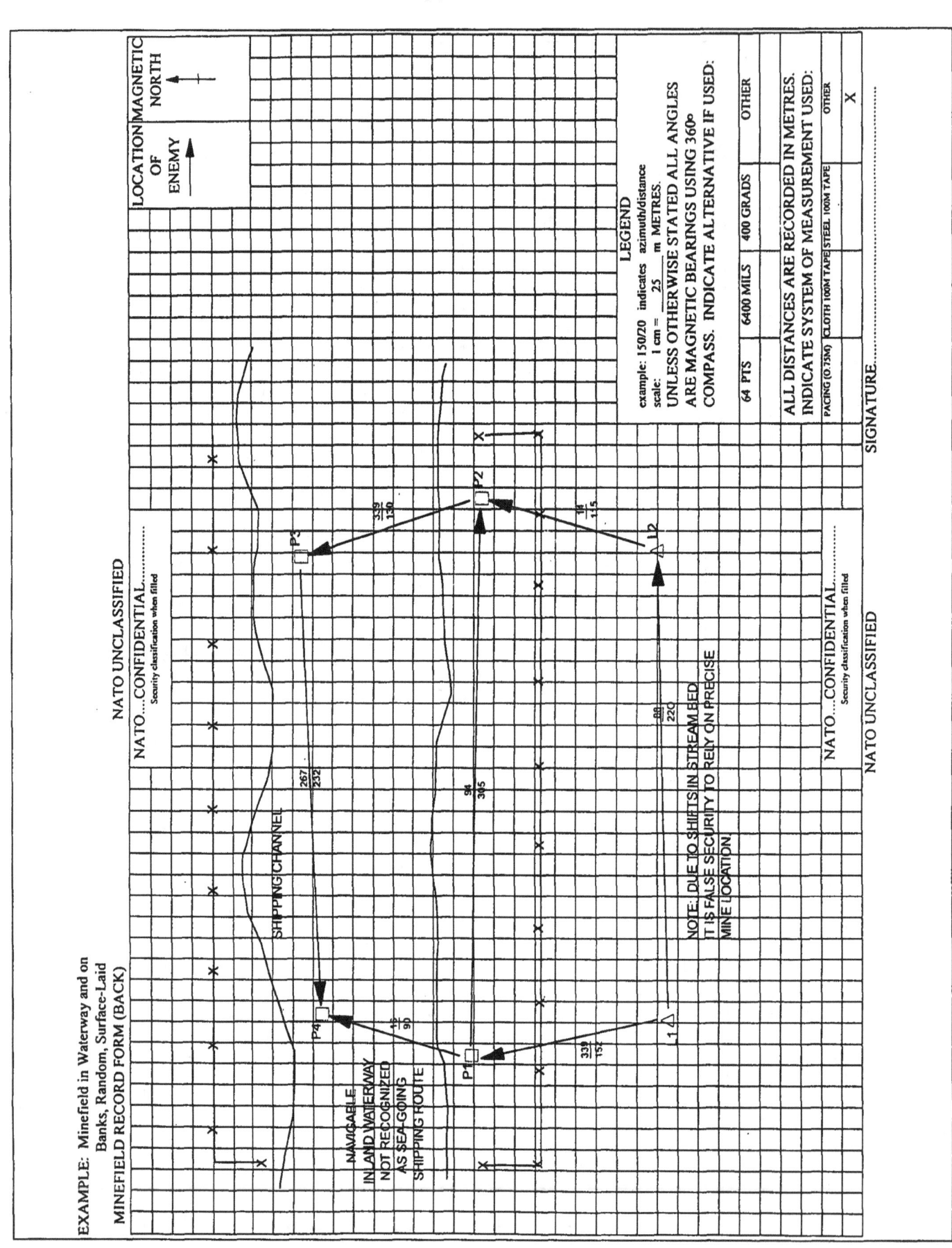

NATO STANAG 2036, Appendix 7 to Annex B

EXAMPLE: Nuisance Minefield, Buried

MINEFIELD RECORD FORM (Front)

NATO UNCLASSIFIED

APPENDIX 7 TO ANNEX B TO STANAG 2036
(Edition 4)

MINEFIELD RECORD

NATO...CONFIDENTIAL......
(Security classification when filled)

COPY ......1...... OF ....5......
SHEET NO .....1...... OF ....1......

MINEFIELD NUMBER: 3/29-INF-12-E
MAP: SERIES, NO AND SCALE: M745, 1:50,000
SHEET NO.(OR NAME): 5560 (ALTST ADT)

		DATE AND TIME	
AUTHORITY: 29 Mech Inf Bde		START: 231400Z Jun	
LAYING UNIT: Co A, 3d Bn		COMPLETION: 231800Z Jun	
OFFICER IN CHARGE: CPT Berger		RECORDER: SGT Runde	

LANDMARKS

NO.	COORDINATES	DESCRIPTION
1	ZZ 37378381	Milestone 50, Road from Village 'Y' to 'Z'
2	ZZ 37438373	Expedient Landmark - 'U' Pickets
3		
4		

INTERMEDIATE MARKERS

NO.	DESCRIPTION
1	
2	
3	
4	

DESCRIPTION OF BOUNDARY FENCE OR MARKING
None used

NO. OF STRIPS/ROWS...... DESCRIPTION OF STRIP/ROW MARKERS:

LANES

NO.	WIDTH	HOW MARKED	METHOD OF CLOSING
1			
2			
3			

NOTES

1. MINE CLUSTERS AT...... METRES/SPACES SPACING......
2. Nuisance. Mining. 'A'.. Landmarks..as. Above.......
3. Nuisance. Mining. 'B'. Boundaries..as.follows:......
......1..15m..West..of. Abutment..(ZZ..383838)......
......2..15m..East.of. Road.Junction...(ZZ..384838)......
......3..10m..On. Both. Sides..of. Road.......
4..Nuisance..Mining..'C'.....Mines..in. a..15m..Radius. Around......
......Centre..of. Junction...(ZZ..374483).......
5..Nuisance. Mining. 'D'..Boundaries..as. follows:......
......P5..ZZ..38388389..... P6...ZZ..38358388......
......P7..ZZ..38378384..... P8...ZZ..38398385......

TACTICAL MINEFIELD / NUISANCE MINEFIELD / PHONEY MINEFIELD

		ANTITANK MINES (AT)									ANTIPERSONNEL MINES								
	IOE	TYPE	TYPE	NO.	TYPE	NO.	TYPE	NO.	TOTAL AT MINES	ANTI LIFT DEV	TYPE	NO.	TYPE	NO.	TYPE	NO.	TYPE	NO.	TOTAL AP MINES
		DM									DM 31								
BURIED AND	A	64							64	6	130								130
	B	120							120	12	180								180
SURFACE LAID	C	40							40	4	75								75
	D	60							60	6									
IN STRIPS	E																		
	F																		
IN ROWS	G																		
W/O PATTERN	H																		
	J																		
TOTAL		284							284	28	385								385

M I N E S (left margin label)

NATO........CONFIDENTIAL......

SIGNATURE (OFFICER IN CHARGE)......
DATE:......23..June79......

NATO UNCLASSIFIED

NATO STANAG 2036, Appendix 7 to Annex B

NATO STANAG 2036, Appendix 7 to Annex B—Continued

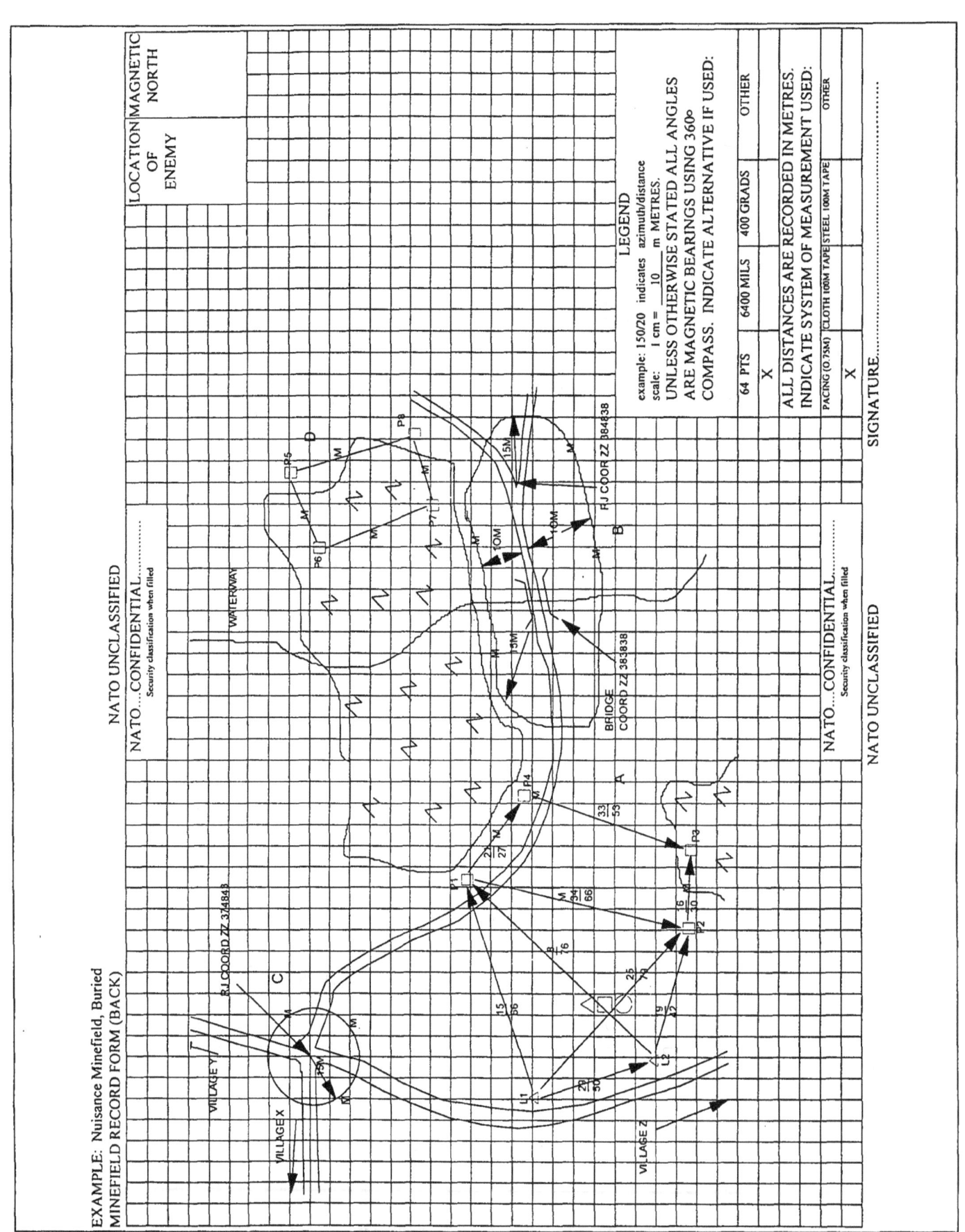

NATO Standardization Agreement (STANAG) 2036 Annex C

ANNEX C TO STANAG 2036 (Edition 4)
SPECIAL INSTRUCTIONS FOR LAYING MINEFIELDS AND PREPARING
MINEFIELD RECORDS

1. When a minefield is changed, a new form will be submitted showing the entire minefield after the change. This does not apply if mines are subsequently dispersed into an existing minefield or when lanes in an existing minefield are closed, in which case the original record will be annotated (see paragraph 19.e. of the STANAG).

2. When "measured-in-whole", the minefield record must contain the following information:

   a. All landmarks and intermediate markers, if used. (A minimum of two land marks will be used.)

   b. Bearings and distances:

      (1) From landmark to its associated intermediate markers.

      (2) From landmarks (or intermediate marker(s)) to nearest strip/row marker.

      (3) From landmarks (or intermediate marker(s))to entrance of lanes (center line).

      (4) For each straight line section of lane(s) (center line).

      (5) From end points of strip/row to end point of the following mine strip/row (in the direction of the enemy).

      (6) For each straight line section of the mine strips/rows and of IOE baseline.

      (7) From end points of forward strip/row to end points of IOE baseline.

      (8) For each short mine strip/row associated with the IOE. The bearing should be measured and recorded from the point of intersection of the short mine strip/row and the IOE baseline.

   c. Locating number and types of stored mines or other means intended to be used for closing lanes.

   d. Approximate location of perimeter fence, or line of warning signs when minefields are not fenced.

   e. Number of mines in each strip or row (or short mine strip in IOE).

   f. Total number of mines of each type.

   g. Number of clusters in each short mine strip in IOE.

   h. Location of mines with antilift devices or tripwire mines if applicable. (Cluster numbers to be entered in notes column.)

   i. Period of effectiveness of mines with special fuzing systems.

NATO Standardization Agreement (STANAG) 2036 Annex C—Continued

3. When "measured-in-part", the minefield record should comprise as much of the following information as possible:

   a. Landmarks and intermediate markers, if required.

   b. Corner points of mined terrain.

   c. Bearings and distances from landmarks via intermediate markers to at least two corner points.

   d. Bearings and distances from corner point to corner point or end point of a mine rov/strip to end point of an adjacent mine row/strip along the outline.

   e. Number and types of mines.

   f. Date/time of termination of minefield effectiveness when using mines equipped with self-neutralizing fuzes.

   g. Approximate location of fencing, or line of warning signs when minefields are not fenced.

4. Nuisance minefields will normally be recorded as described in paragraph 3 above. The extent of nuisance minefields around a prominent landmark will be designated by giving the radius in meters together with the grid reference of the landmark. Elongated nuisance minefields will be designated by giving the grid references of the end points and their widths in meters. Information on numbers and types of mines, as well as on the time of effectiveness, is required.

5. The following symbols will be used when markers/points are shown on the minefield diagram:

   a. Landmark/Intermediate marker.

   b. End point/corner point or Lane entrance/Lane exit.

   c. Turning point.

· APPENDIX B

References and Related Publications

Joint Publications

Joint Pub 3-0   Doctrine for Joint Operations

Marine Corps Publications

Fleet Marine Force Manuals (FMFMs)

FMFM 3-1   Command and Staff Action
FMFM 13   MAGTF Engineer Operations
FMFM 13-7   MAGTF Breaching Operations

Marine Corps Reference Publications (MCRPs)

MCRP 4-25.5   Bulk Liquids Operations

Army Publications

U.S. Army Field Manuals (FMs)

FM 5-15   Field Fortification
FM 5-34   Engineer Field Data
FM 5-36   Route Reconnaissance and Classification
FM 5-100   Engineer Combat Operations
FM 5-101   Mobility
FM 5-102   Countermobility
FM 5-103   Survivability
FM 5-104   General Engineering
FM 5-250   Explosives and Demolitions
FM 6-20-40   Tactics, Techniques, and Procedures for Fire Support for Brigade Operations (Heavy)
FM 6-20-50   Tactics, Techniques, and Procedures for Fire Support for Brigade Operations (Light)
FM 10-52   Water Supply in Theaters of Operation
FM 20-32   Mine/Countermine Operations

Department of the Army Forms (DA Forms)

DA Form 1248   Road Reconnaissance Report
DA Form 1249   Bridge Reconnaissance Report
DA Form 1250   Tunnel Reconnaissance Report
DA Form 1251   Ford Reconnaissance Report
DA Form 1252   Ferry Reconnaissance Report
DA Form 1355   Minefield Record
DA Form 1711-R Engineer Reconnaissance Report
DA Form 2203-R Demolition Reconnaissance Report
DA Form 5032-R Field Artillery Delivered Minefield Planning Sheet

North Atlantic Treaty Organization (NATO) Publications

STANAG 2036   Land Minefield Laying, Marking, Recording and Reporting Procedures

The following list contains a brief description, the length, and current edition date of NATO Standardization Agreements (STANAGs), Allied Technical Publications (ATPs), Allied Ordnance Publications (AOPs), and Allied Administrative Publications (AAPs) that are of interest to engineers but are not included because of their size or infrequent use.

NATO STANAGs

2010, *Military Load Classification Markings*, provides standardized system of marking the military load classification of bridges, rafts, and vehicles; 10 pages; July 1994.

2017, *Orders to the Demolition Guard Commander and Demolition Firing Party Commander (Non Nuclear)*, provides standardized procedures to the Demolition Guard Commander and to the Demolition Firing Party Commander in connection with the preparation, charging, and firing of non-nuclear demolitions in operations on land; 14 pages; July 1981.

2021, *Military Computation of Bridge, Ferry, Raft, and Vehicle Classifications*, provides instructions, charts, and graphs for calculating the load carrying capacity of bridges, ferries, and rafts and load effects of vehicles; 40 pages; September 1990.

2096, *Reporting Engineer Information in the Field*, provides standardized minimum engineer reporting requirements to be used by the NATO forces to ensure an adequate flow of engineer information during operations; 17 pages; January 1988.

2123, *Obstacle Folder*, provides standardized procedures to be used by the NATO nations in connection with the preparation in peacetime of preplanned, preconstructed and/or field-type obstacle; 35 pages; November 1984.

2136, *Minimum Standards of Water Potability*, provides criteria to standardize water potabiltiy between military organizations. It also provides a list of water treatment equipment used by 14 NATO nations; 25 pages; December 1985.

2321, *The NATO Code of Colours for Identification of Ammunition (Except Ammunition of a Calibre Below 20 mm*, provides color coding criteria as indicated in the title, a listing of items to which the color coding does not apply, and color code identification charts; 10 pages; March 1993.

2394, *Land Force Combat Engineer Doctrine*, contains only the agreement to utilize the basic document ATP-52, *Land Force Combat Engineer Doctrine*; January 1993.

2395, *Opposed Water Crossing Procedures*, Standardizes procedures for conducting an opposed water in a forward combat area. It covers the following information: stages/phases, forces, critical functions, movement control responsibilities, engineer tasks, responsibilities of the crossing unit, communications and combat service support responsibilities, the crossing plan, terms and definitions, and charts showing the sequence of crossing events; 14 pages; September 1991.

2818, *Characteristics of Demolition Accessories to Determine Their Operational Interchangeability*, provides characteristics of demolitions materials used by various NATO members, as well as a general discussion of demolition principles. It also provides instructions for conducting comparison tests to evaluate the compatibility of foreign demolition materials; 188 pages; May 1979.

2885, *Emergency Supply of Water in War*, provides procedures to standardize the emergency supply of water to NATO forces if the public water supply breaks down. It contains information pertaining to: definitions, requirements, quality and quantity, impurities, responsibilities, water sources, storage, distribution, and treatment methods; 32 pages; November 1990.

2889, *Marking of Hazardous Areas and Routes Through Them*, provides instructions to standardize procedures to mark hazardous areas on land and those routes through or between them. It discusses requirements, types of marking, definitions, and methods and procedures for marking various types of areas; 15 pages; February 1990.

2933, *Land Forces Explosives and Demolition Accessories Interchangeability Catalog in Wartime*, contains only the agreement to use the basic document AOP-19, *Land Forces Explosives and Demolition Accessories Interchangeability Catalog in Wartime*; September 1993.

2963, *Coordination of Field Artillery Scatterable Mines*, provides procedures to call for artillery-delivered scatterable mine missions from the forces of other NATO nations by using standard calls, terms, procedures, and commands. It discusses employment, coordination, request procedures, reporting and planning data, and charts; 24 pages; September 1992.

2989, *Transfer of Barriers*, outlines the procedures to be used by the NATO forces for the transfer of barriers between military forces of different nationalities. It contains the major considerations of barriers and detailed procedures to successfully transfer the barrier; 40 pages; January 1985.

2990, *Principles and Procedures for the Employment in Land Warfare of Scatterable Mines with a Limited Laid Life*, contains only the agreement to use basic document ATP-50, *Principles and procedures for the Employment in Land Warfare of Scatterable Mines with a limited Laid Life*, including change 2; September 1995.

2991, *NATO Combat Engineer Glossary*, contains only the agreement to use the basic document AAP-19(B), *NATO Combat Engineer Glossary*; October 1993.

Allied Publications

Allied Technical Publications

ATP-50, *Principles and Procedures for the Employment in Land Warfare of Scatterable Mines with a Limited Laid Life*, provides standardized principles and procedures to be used by NATO forces when employing scatterable mines with a limited laid life in land warfare; 4 pages; September 1995.

ATP-52, *Land Force Combat Engineer Doctrine*, provides NATO combat engineer doctrine in the following areas: the role of combat engineers, principles of employment, tasks in battle, defensive operations, delaying operations, offensive operations, transitional phases, and special operations; 126 pages; February 1993.

Allied Ordnance Publication

AOP-19, *Land Forces Explosives and Demolition Accessories Interchangeability Catalog in Wartime*, provides a catalog of explosives and demolition items used by NATO forces, and shows which can be interchanged and used by each nation during wartime. It is not intended for use in training or peacetime operations. It provides, where necessary, additional data, limitations, and/or clarifying information required for use of such materials. The following information is provided for each item: NATO ammunition demand/reporting code, generic description, NATO stock number, national abbreviation and short code, quantity of issue, particular characteristics, and remarks; 55 pages; September 1993.

Allied Administrative Publication

AAP-19(B), *NATO Combat Engineer Glossary*, provides a glossary of terms and definitions of engineer significance in both English and French languages; 48 pages; October 1993.